Concerning the Rites of Psychoanalysis

T0327002

To my mother
who left
at this turning point of my labyrinth

Concerning the Rites of Psychoanalysis

Or the Villa of the Mysteries

Bice Benvenuto

Polity Press

Copyright © Bice Benvenuto 1994

The right of Bice Benvenuto to be identified as author of this work has been asserted in accordance with the Copyright, Designs and Patents Act 1988.

First published in 1994 by Polity Press in association with Blackwell Publishers.

Reprinted 2006

Polity Press
65 Bridge Street
Cambridge CB2 1UR, UK

Polity Press
350 Main Street
Malden, MA 02148, USA

ISBN 0 7456 1249 0
ISBN 0 7456 1530 9 (pbk)

A CIP catalogue record for this book is available from the British Library.

Typeset in 10½ on 12½ pt Palatino by Best-set Typesetter Ltd., Hong Kong
Printed and bound in Great Britain by Marston Book Services Limited, Oxford

This book is printed on acid-free paper.

For further information on Polity, visit our website: www.polity.co.uk

Contents

Part IV   127

Acknowledgements

My acknowledgements go first to all my analysands and students whose patience towards me as analyst and teacher made it possible for me to write this book; to Parveen Adams, who first encouraged me into this enterprise, and to Teresa Brennan, who was the midwife of it in the best Socratic tradition; and to my brother, Sergio Benvenuto, who encouraged my first steps into psychoanalysis. To my friends Wilma Aiello and Dominique Ducos goes my gratitude for their untiring faith in my efforts, which otherwise might have failed me. I wish to thank James Greene and Adalberto Mecarelli for their artistic assistance; and F.D.C. Archibald, Desmond Scott and Bruno Zarri for their technical assistance. Many thanks to David Held and Elizabeth Wright for their encouraging comments and suggestions.

Some of the material in 'Compliance and Disagreement' (chapter 5) has already been published in 'Sexual Difference', ed. Robert J.C. Young, *Oxford Literary Review* 8 (1986) pp. 28–34, © 1986 *Oxford Literary Review*. An Italian version of 'The Passion of Childhood' (chapter 3) has been published in *Psicoterapia e Scienze Umane* (Milan). An earlier version of Interlude was published in *Topoi. An International Review of Philosophy*, Vol. 12, No. 2, September 1993. Plates 5 and 6 are reproduced by kind permission of Scala, Florence. All other photographs are by Umberto Telesco.

A true lover is proved such by his pain of heart;
No sickness is there like sickness of heart.
The lover's ailment is different from all ailments;
Love is the astrolabe of God's mysteries.
A lover may hanker after this love or that love,
But at the last he is drawn to the King of love.
However much we describe and explain love,
When we fall in love we are ashamed of our words.
Explanation by the tongue makes most things clear,
But love unexplained is clearer.
When pen hasted to write,
On reaching the subject of love it split in twain.
When the discourse touched on the matter of love,
Pen was broken and paper torn.
In explaining it Reason sticks fast, as an ass in mire;
Naught but Love itself can explain love and Lovers!

Reprinted from *Teachings of Rumi* (published by the Octagon Press Ltd, London 1979).

Preface

This book is not a comprehensive commentary on some of Lacan's concepts, nor yet another introduction to his work. Still, it may cover some of those two functions, in so far as speaking 'Lacanian' in Britain is not the same as speaking 'Lacanian' in France or in South America. Lacan in English is always a sort of cultural translation of a vision of the world rather than of specific terms and concepts which, nevertheless, can be taken for granted in One culture and dismissed in the Other. The One and the Other will in fact be the main characters of this book. It will be their battlefield, as well as providing the possibility of an encounter.

The book's foundation lay in seminars and lectures I have given over the last years to heterogeneous audiences. Just as the analysand's free associations are revealed as neither free nor random in the analytic process, so were my papers. Yet when I re-read the first paper I wrote six years ago, I found to my great surprise that all the things, all the threads which had led me to the last piece of work on shame which I had just written were already there, ready for me to develop or struggle with. I did not know then, that, like the first session in an analysis, all the key elements were presented, but without elaboration, in a condensed and obscure way.

What came out in the end from these papers is this book. But they were already linked by a train of thought which constantly led me to a few *idées fixes* which I have approximately bound together in the four parts of this book.

In part I, I try to unfold my questioning about the psychoanalytic process and its relation to other practices, now and in the past, which claim healing effects on the human soul, such as the religious *cura animae* and the philosophical *cura sui*. The common denominator which struck me first was that they are all practices of love: love for knowledge in philosophy, God's love in mysticism, and transference love in psychoanalysis. Then I traced my steps back to Plato, for whom love is already a matter of knowledge, and to pagan religiosity, and especially the Dionysiac cult, which from ancient Greece spread into the Roman culture in different ways. These are the Dionysiac mysteries, which were characterized by their initiatory rites. Their enigmatic representation is found in the Villa of the Mysteries at Pompeii where a frescoed room represents the process of the unveiling of the Phallus. I have borrowed the idea of these ancient rites because they illustrate well the analytical progression, which is evocative and revealing at the same time. In both practices there is a work of unveiling of both our past and what we will know always a moment too late, our destiny. But we find out our destiny only by acknowledging the steps already made which lead to its conclusion. And both psychoanalytical and mysteric rites are about how to accomplish one's own 'destiny' through a process of undressing and unveiling, of dejection and resurrection, which is typical of all rites of passage. But unlike mystical initiation, which aims at an esoteric revelation for only the few, rites of passage do not initiate to a 'beyond', but to life itself: how to carry on living meaningfully with and in spite of an unknown 'beyond', how to go through the necessary initiation into being human. We are introduced into the human bond through rites of passage. They integrate the initiate into the mysteries of the symbolic world, such as having a name which bonds to others, without getting lost among them. Anthropologists know this very well in relation to other cultures.[1] But we have our own rites of passage: religious cults (circumcision, baptism, communion, etc.), social progressions (schooling, degrees, qualifications and promotions), and last, but not least, psychoanalysis, which offers a process that the other two are no longer able to direct. The rite of passage that psychoanalysis offers is the Oedipal myth and its possible (and impossible) solutions. Some clinical material will illustrate some of the relations between knowledge and love as well as passion and madness, which are part and parcel of any unveiling rite.

In part II, I will approach the 'mystery' of psychoanalysis: the woman and her sexuality. Dora will be our guide through our tour into hysteria, this paradigm of women's paradoxes in attempting to have a symbolic position in the social bond. We will see how the Dionysiac rites epitomize the struggle of sacred and profane love as a symbolic initiation into womanhood and feminine sexuality. This same struggle between sacred and profane entangles hysteric women (and men) in a perpetual conflict within themselves. With the radical split between earthly and divine which monotheism introduced, we have lost the symbolic rites for womanhood. Marriage and motherhood have become meaningless vestiges of women's ancient initiations. Freud, who realized the curative effects of myths and of rites of passage, brought up to date for the contemporary age the myth of Oedipus as a moment of passage from polymorphous infantile sexuality into sexual differentiation. But if the rite of castration seems to work for the boy, the question is whether it works as well for the girl. Freud had to admit that the girl will never find a solution to her Oedipus. She will stay there, in a never-accomplished rite of passage.

In part III, I will dwell on another mystery of psychoanalysis: the mystery of origins. Child analysis is not just an analytical specialization or technique but a field of theoretical development into earlier and earlier stages of infancy. Its attempts to find a point of origin for psychic development affected the theory and the practice of psychoanalysis at large. I will comment on three famous cases drawn from child analysis literature, all concerning a childhood phobia. My commentary on Freud's little Hans, Winnicott's 'Piggle' and Klein's *Narrative of a Child Analysis* will try to determine their different ways of leading the psychoanalytical rite of the Oedipal myth. All three analysts interpret and direct the treatments around the axes of Oedipal anxieties, but I will show how in each case Oedipus works at different levels. Whereas Freud introduces the myth by recounting it to Hans, like a tale, Winnicott does not articulate it, but rather acts it, plays it with the little girl who will in this way verbalize the 'nascent unconscious' in terms of transference. I try to read, with Winnicott, his masterfully directed sessions as they unfold in his notes. In the approach that Klein takes in Richard's case I try to come to grips with the theoretical consequences of the Kleinian concept of an early Oedipus complex, and her use of it in her *furor interpretandi*.

In part IV, I will try to draw away the last veil of the analytical and mysteric undressing, only to find ourselves face to face with the 'demon of shame'. Shame appears in the Dionysiac frescos at the point of the unveiling of the phallus. But such an unveiling is never fully achieved because, even in those times, the phallus showed itself only as modestly veiled. A clinical case will illustrate how knowledge unveils shame not only for one's own ignorance, but also for one's own nakedness and mortality. Shame is the feeling that dictates modesty, which is the state of mind attendant on any initiation, whereas 'to die of shame' is the neurotic version of one's own relation not only to sexuality but to death as well.

A Note on the Ancient Mysteries

I was born in a place where the earth trembles,[1] but its inhabitants no longer notice it. This place is dominated by a volcano on whose slopes rests an ancient Roman town once buried under its lava, subsequently brought to light again in the stillness of its ruins. On the edge of the unearthed town there is a Roman villa called 'the Villa of the Mysteries', which still imposes a perturbed silence on its visitors.

A little further down the coast you can smell the sulphur from the volcanic boiling earth. In this area is a little fishing village, now being deserted because of bradyseisms which announce a new piece of land kicking under the sea. Seismologists can do as little about these phenomena as anyone could at the time of Pompeii. A sense of poverty, fatalism, unruliness and artistry characterizes the people of that strip of land.

And here I am, far from the place of my origins, able to write about these phenomena not only as a geological symptom, but as my own. This unruly land could also be used as a wider metaphor for the unconscious itself, as the place where we were all born but without knowing it. It is exactly the mystery of this unknown that both Dionysiac rites and psychoanalysis deal with.

On a first visit to the fresco room of the Villa of the Mysteries in Pompeii, one first feels oneself to be an intruder. The action is already in progress. One has no place in the hyper-realistic living picture among figures slightly more than human size. The Villa's walls depict several happenings taking place at the same time. All the walls are telling the visitor something, addressing one with equal force. Finding one's bearings again, one looks for a chronological point of reference. The visitor wants to start somewhere. And by the time one chooses where to start, one finds oneself already caught in the initiatory sequence. When one comes in front of the 'terrified' face and posture of the initiate who is instinctively running away from it all (plate 4), one comes to the realization that either one is involved, one is not a spectator, or one wants to take flight, like the initiate. In the Villa the visitor experiences some obscure emotions; one does not know what they are about.

I shall start where I chose to start the first time I saw these frescos: the sequence on the left-hand side from the entrance.

The first figure is Domina (plate 1), the matron of the house, priestess and mother. There are two different ways of positioning her. One theory puts her at the end of the initiation rites sequel. Toynbee (1929) believes that the 'matronly woman seated on a couch' is the initiate herself after the wedding has been performed. According to this interpretation the whole ritual is a reproduction from a pre-nuptial rite 'for women only' in Demeter's or Kore's sanctuary. She is the bride seated while waiting to meet her bridegroom. For other commentators she is the Domina of the house where such Dionysiac rituals took place. According to Macchioro (1920) the villa was a private and secret Orphic basilica, and for Maiuri (1931) the priestess is the one who introduces and presides over the rituals as the host of a sanctuary which is also her house.

In any case Domina was not an unusual character in the Campania region. She was a priestess who often initiated her own children. The mysteries, imported from Greek cults, became very popular in Rome, to the point where the Bacchanalia had to be banned in 186 BC as they were in contrast with the austerity of Roman family customs. And then a variety of secret associations practising the mysteries sprang up, especially in the south of Italy in their esoteric form, which the Pompeian room conveys. It is important to stress the Orphic origins of Dionysiac mysteries,[2] which were practised by limited circles of philosophers and intellectuals in Roman times.[3] In her function of initiator of the 'knowledgeable', the Roman Domina resembles the Greek Diotima, Socrates' initiator.[4]

After Matrona, who has been seen as both spectator and director of the play, a veiled woman enters the scene and stops to listen to a child who is reading under the guidance of a woman, perhaps his initiated mother (plate 2). The child is one of those sacred youths assigned to be ministers at the service of Dionysus. Or is he 'Dionysus mystes' himself, reading the ritual of the sacred text under the guidance of his mother Demeter or Kore/Persephone?[5]

After one scene (plate 3) in which a priestess is both veiling and unveiling a laurel twig as part of the regalia and another two scenes where half-animal, half-human bodies feature (Silenus, satyrs and Pan), we witness, suddenly, the initiate's panic (plate 4). Many interpretations have been expounded concerning the 'terrified woman', all of them referring to the cause of terror somewhere else in the fresco. Some ascribe her terror to the next scene, others to the torments taking place on the wall in front of her. But I would rather see the preceding Pan scene as the 'cause' of her panic. Pan is the god of panic as well as of rural delight. Pan, in Greek, also means 'the all', the personification of all aspects of nature, including orgiastic manifestations of maternity (Pan's woman is shown suckling a goat) and feminine sexuality. What is the wealthily dressed woman terrified of? Of what she sees in front or, as well, of what comes before? Could the scene of terror arise from the god Pan's peaceful country scene, in that the source of her panic is the lost union of nature and the human?[6] So, after preparatory rites and libation, the initiate is put to her first test, and her impulse to flee is the first dramatic phase of the action so far.

Nor do good omens come in the divination of the next scene (plate 5) where the monstrous mask held up by a satyr and reflected in a metallic cup breaks the narcissistic mirror image.[7] The old Silenus is predicting possibly the whipping coming in one of the next frescos.

In the fifth scene we come to the divine couple (plate 5), broken image too, but by the accidents of time. Maiuri sees it this way:

> Detached yet still connected with the rest, absorbed in the bliss of an amorous embrace, the divine couple does not seem to be in touch with what is going on around them. Dionysus and his bride Ariadne are present divinities, and already projected in the non-human vision of divinity. They are the emblem of the ultramundane blessedness which the initiate can reach only through the tests and the martyrdom of the Mysteries. The ecstatic abandon of Dionysus and what is still his partner's austere mantled bearing, this tells us that we are in the moment which precedes the nuptial rite. In the god already drunk on wine and love and in the woman who embraces him is already

expressed the desired joy of the nuptial embrace.[8] (Maiuri, 1931, pp. 148–50: my translation)

Even if we embrace the explanation of a special initiatory rite before nuptials only for women, performed in a sanctuary devoted to Demeter and her daughter Kore/Persephone, Dionysus' mother, this would not contradict the fact that Dionysus was initiated into his mother's Eleusinian mysteries. So that, in either case, the frescos could be representing, consciously or not, the initiation of Dionysus himself by his mother rather than his wife Ariadne, and both transmission of or continuity between Eleusinian rites and the Dionysiac ones. Most of all, this is striking for a psychoanalyst because something of repressed mother–son incest seems to be at play in the presumed continuity of the Eleusinian–Dionysiac mysteries.[9] What they have in common is reaching ecstasy by means of sexual union, a rite whose only parallel lies in the East, in Tantra's sexual practices.[10]

It is at this ecstatic point that the most sacred action takes place in the sixth scene (plate 6): the unveiling of the phallus. An initiate kneels down and lifts the veil of the basket containing the emblems generating fecundity. One catches a glimpse of the phallus behind the veil. The phallus *almost* appears, between ecstasy and shame, when suddenly a whip prevents the culmination of the action of unveiling. A winged feminine divinity, Aidos, demon of shame, suddenly appears with the sound of her whip.[11] This time it is not the initiate desiring to flee from the horrific sight, but shame barring the woman's sight by means of violence.[12]

This takes us to the seventh scene, the whipped woman and the Bacchant (plate 7). What is the cause of her shamed paleness? Is it because of her sterility? Or is it the expression of feminine suffering in ancient art before Christianity portrayed it in the Virgin's Pietà? Or shame because of the manifestation of her masochistic enjoyment? We do not know, but we can only see that out of shame springs the dancing nude, a transfiguration of the polymorphous perverse into a Bacchant. Is this the transformation of the masochistic phantasy into raving pleasure? Again we can only see that our Pompeian initiate, who has been through the mystery of incestuous divine union, the revelation of the phallus, and the shameful for-bidding of such a revelation, finds herself not in an ineffable or transcendental state but in one of joyful intoxication.[13]

But the story does not end there. A window separates the Bacchant from the next scene (plate 8). This is the nuptial dressing where the initiate gets ready for the symbolic marriage with the god. Helped by a maiden, she is doing her hair while a little Eros holds up a mirror for her. Her ringed eyes, on a face which expresses the post-ecstatic serenity following important events, is voluptuous. On the other side of the corner of the wall another Eros watches the scene while waiting for the bride to prepare herself with modesty (recomposition of the broken mirror image).

We are back at the main entrance, and can indulge for a moment the speculation hinted at by a guide: that the villa was probably Pompeii's brothel and Domina its mistress. Maybe the guide was not so far from the uncanny fact that sexual images and evocations need not differ much from sacred ones.[14]

But what has psychoanalysis to do with this contiguity of sacred and profane, sexuality and initiation?

Lacan in 1949 ended his renowned paper on the Mirror Stage in this enigmatic way (1977d, p. 7): 'Psychoanalysis may accompany the patient to the ecstatic limit of the "Thou art that", in which is revealed to him the cipher of his mortal destiny, but it is not in our mere power as practitioners to bring him to that point where the real journey begins'. It was only when I got hold of his last unpublished seminar, 'La topologie et le temps' (1979), that something like a solution to a rebus came to my mind. Can one guess what he was talking about in his last seminar one year before his death? He was talking about the end of analysis. He had come full circle back to the last sentence of his Mirror Stage where the end of analysis does not have to coincide with 'the point where the real journey begins'.

Psychoanalysis is only the *accompaniment* to the ecstatic moment, the simple limit of 'Thou art that', in your human destiny. Psychoanalysis is not mysticism. The 'beyond' is not its stake. Mysticism aims at the encounter with the 'ineffable', with the divine. This is the ethics of mysticism and not of psychoanalysis, which does not aim at achieving a mystic union. But neither do the Dionysiac rites of the Pompeian frescos. Like psychoanalysis they describe a progression which includes all our demons and sacred encounters. But their aim was the healing of the souls, an initiation to our everyday life via a god. Psychoanalytical practice too is a progression of encounters with demons and lost paradises. They are both processes of unveiling and revelation. Unveiling *is* the ethics for both processes, where it is its action that cures. To aim at an ideal or standard cure, be it the union with god or the end of an endless headache, is not the business of psychoanalysis. And still . . .

Part I

1

A Discourse on Love

And still I wonder if a discourse on love, whether mystical or earthly, is possible at all. For the ancients, it was part of the initiatory rites in the quest for knowledge, but today? Is it possible at all if we include the wide range of heterogeneous phenomena, such as falling in love, romantic love, making love, lustful love, sentiments, passion, desire, maternal love, love for knowledge, divine love, and so forth? Have all these types of love something in common apart from the word which designates them? Is there something we call love which is immediately recognizable in whatever form it presents itself, be it in the form of tenderness or of a crime of passion?

Roland Barthes in his fragments of *A Lover's Discourse* (1978) could not find a better way to approach love than by trying to grasp its signs in the fragmentary and contradictory set of images, gestures and hidden messages and emotions through which a lover speaks; that is, by grasping love as it emerges through discourse. But even though discourse and the phenomenology of love seem to coincide, the latter can only be recognized as love, says Barthes in the preface of the book, if you already know what the 'amorous feeling' is: this feeling which will never be mentioned again in his text. Love remains the lover's unspeakable datum.

So if we adopt Barthes's assumptions, we can legitimately say that all we know about love is its discourse, and that you cannot recognize it if you do not already know the amorous feeling, which, of course, he does not tell us anything about. This feeling constitutes an x, the incognito of love's discourse, which surrounds its own riddle in a code, which reveals and hides its own content. But only a supposed one, because we could not give thus far any evidence of such a content.

Some could protest that a discourse is always a discourse on something, that it must have a referent and, if nothing else, we must be referring to an irreducible feeling. Still, as we have already pointed out, we experience love through so many different feelings that we can state that it never appears in its irreducible essence. Whereas it can be evoked or even known, in the way Barthes suggests in his preface, it cannot be defined. What can one say about a feeling? Many analysts insist on wanting to grasp, interpret and communicate their patient's feelings from what they are saying or doing. On the other hand Barthes attempts an X-ray of a lover's feeling by not saying what it is; it is the lover's discourse that will evoke and provoke such a feeling.

Literary work, like psychoanalytic work, effects knowledge (*savoir*).[1] Transference is love for the analyst not as an object of desire, but as its cause because s/he has functioned as an *agent provocateur*, and her/his position of supposed knowledge pushes the analysand closer to a relation to a supposed 'original' love-object. The analyst who pretends to know how the other feels surely provokes an outpouring of feelings upon her/himself, where the analysand is only responding to the analyst's appeal to feel; that is, to her/his suggestion. In that case the analysand will be responding to the analyst's discourse on love.

Love and sexuality

What am I going to write about the feeling of love, then, if it can be 'known' and evoked but not defined? All I can do, perhaps, is write a discourse on the discourse of love. At least love speaks; that is enough to start with. It does not say the undefinable x, but it might say something about it in code, provided it remains clandestine. Definitions of love abound, of course, but that which is indicted in the 'legality' of language is the enjoyment which pertains to it: the erotic enjoyment. But in what sense is enjoyment left out of language if, as a matter of fact, we talk a lot and easily about sexual enjoyment: in the arts, in science, in jokes, in various counselling settings? We cannot deny that sex is the star of the media. Take, for example, sexual counselling and education: here, unlike jokes which aim at the obscene, the aim is a socially integrable sexuality, safe and happy sex. The emphasis is on the achievement of a good and healthy orgasm as the ultimate goal; that is all that sexual enjoyment wants, after all. Here one aspect or part of enjoyment is taken for the whole. But is there a whole Eros? Certainly healthy sex is only a part of it, and more precisely that part which coincides with one of the operations of language itself: namely, to restrict erotic indecency within reassuring and objectifying linguistic schemata about sex. Sexual enjoyment is that which sexual education leaves out in its enlightenments, the last and most difficult thing to tell children, even after Freud told us that children know it without being allowed to. Maybe children are innocent as long as they are allowed to be innocent, for as long as prohibition coincides with silence: what else is repression if not this impossibility of articulation?[2]

The case of little Hans is paradigmatic here (Freud, 1909):[3] according to Freud, Hans's father was failing because, in spite of his enlightened methods of upbringing (the light being that of psychoanalysis), he could not enlighten his son on the existence of the vagina and coitus even when instructed to do so by Freud himself. The child's first attempt to articulate sexuality, which is the crux of the Oedipus theory, was met by a lack of articulation on the side of the father. Do children get ill if their parents do not articulate sexuality for them? In a way they do, as the articulation of sexuality in the Oedipal process takes place in the form of a prohibition, the prohibition of incest. To elaborate and establish such a prohibition is the work of the 'latency period'. It is usually only later on, around adolescence, that, in spite of all the restrictions put on sexuality, both from our own repression and from the social order, we encounter sexuality again, and often no less dramatically. The encounter with Mr K.'s sexuality was a traumatic event for Dora, who held desperately onto her latency period elaborations around feminine sexuality: virginity and feminine idealization. [4] In other cases, when all goes well, one happens to come . . . to enjoy sex. In other words, we teach our children to love, not to make love. This view does not contradict the possibility of child abuse; maybe the two aspects go hand in hand. The abuse, after all, takes place in silence.

Until the so-called sexual revolution of the sixties, pleasure and love were commonly assumed to be antinomic phenomena. This antinomy was well expressed by the sexy images in Roger Vadim's films, in which Brigitte Bardot starred as the object of desire whose pursuit drove man adrift. With Eros one slipped off the right path, as it were, into the outlawed field of sex. This took place against the Freudian background of this century's biggest new shift in sexuality, to use Foucault's terms. William Reich (1973) laid down the basis for a change of discourse on sexuality and love which is the precursor of today's hygienic conception of sexuality, of which Aids is the ultimate product. Reich's attempt was to bring together the two phenomena as two aspects of the one and the same: pleasure and orgasm presuppose mental health and, as a consequence of it, a capacity to love. The ideology of free love rose from this fundamental permission *vis-à-vis* a complementarity of love and sex. We read in Reich the past echoes of our pre-HIV sexual policy: that sex is good for love.

Or is it too good for love, for our daily human reassuring love? Reich's sexuality is reassuring. He makes sex fall completely under the sway of the life drive. This is, pushed to its extreme, Freud's equation of Eros and the life drive. But in spite of the Reichian healthy coincidence between Eros and life, people still enter various kinds of consulting room complaining precisely of this, that these two aspects of love do not coincide. They feel cheated. Something about sex and love has not worked: it is one thing to make love, another to love. And this disjunction is so insistent in the analytical experience that psychoanalysis can rightly consider love its speciality, its job, as it were. Psychoanalysis, like Barthes's text, works mainly with the lover's discourse. It works on transference love.

Lacan, whose language was baroque but certainly not romantic, complained in his seminar on transference (1991a) about the fact that only to analysts are their own charms an inconvenience, for the analytical relationship is already 'a bed of love'. According to Lacan, in fact, the analyst is less concerned with the supposed 'good' of the patient than with her/his Eros, as the analysand always turns into a lover in the transference, and the analytical couch turns into a place where the unhappy lover can let his/her Eros speak. It is through transference that we realize all the barriers, threats and fears associated with Eros. In transference an erotic resistance takes place. I say erotic since this is the one side of transference love which resists, which reveals itself only through its own banishment. Transference is, therefore, banned love, but also love for that which is banned from our knowledge. Transference is love for knowledge about what cannot decently be said: our erotic attachment to our parents and its catastrophic consequences. So what is banned is brought forth by transference. It resists, while enacting this very resistance. This is the motor of psychoanalysis.

With Lacan we move away from the Reichian harmony between Eros and life and get closer to the way literature approaches love.

In tragic, courtly, romantic and erotic art, love generally shows itself in two dichotomic aspects: redemption and salvation on the one hand, and on the other, love's more or less subtly ineluctable dangers. The radical manifestations of love in art seem to overrun any ethical code. Love has a code of its own, which borders on the a-ethical; it borders on *jouissance*. [5] This side of love, which is always condemned, even in our sex-hygienic society, pertains to sexual enjoyment, which does not know the limits of decency. In sexual enjoyment the subject loses momentarily the mastery of his/her ego-image. A fragmentariness, a discontinuity, a fading away of the subject takes place, s/he becomes invisible to her/himself in order to enjoy her/his own indecency and the other's. On the other hand the ego-image which gets lost in the amorous destitution can be found again in the beauty and fullness of the lover; s/he becomes the mirror in which we see reflected our lost image. The one who loves is humble, but humble against a background of narcissism. Love appears here in its imaginary glow as that which rescues us from the silent obscurity of sex.

Eros

Freud is close to this idea that love rescues when he claims that Eros is the cohesiveness of life. Freud opposed Thanatos, the death drive, to Eros. For Freud, Eros is, therefore, life; and even more, life in its essence of cohesiviness, which he explained in biological terms, as the connection of cells and their coming together into a common structure that prolongs life. So for Freud the erotic drive attends to this function of life and cohesion, well represented in the effect of reproduction.

> The id, guided by the pleasure principle – that is, by the perception of unpleasure – fends off these tensions in various ways. It does so in the

first place by complying as swiftly as possible with the demands of the non-desexualized libido – by striving for the satisfaction of the directly sexual trends. But it does so in a far more comprehensive fashion in relation to one particular form of satisfaction in which all component demands converge – by discharge of the sexual substances, which are *saturated* vehicles, so to speak, of the erotic tensions. The ejection of the sexual substances in the sexual act corresponds in a sense to the separation of soma and germ-plasm. This accounts for the likeness of the condition that follows complete sexual satisfaction to dying, and for the fact that death coincides with the act of copulation in some of the lower animals. These creatures die in the act of reproduction because, after Eros has been eliminated through the process of satisfaction, *the death instinct has a free hand for accomplishing its purposes.* (Freud, 1923, p. 47: my italics)

So if reproduction is an effect of Eros, it is not its aim, since, on the contrary, it is death which has a free hand in the subject's saturated erotic tensions. The incomprehensible erotic flow does not lead to an essence of life, but on the contrary, to a mere ex-tension of a tension, (an ex-one, the one exhausted in the act of love). Freud again:

both the instincts would be conservative in the strictest sense of the word, since both would be endeavouring to re-establish a state of things that was disturbed by the emergence of life. *The emergence of life would thus be the cause of the continuance of life and also at the same time of the striving towards death; and life itself would be a conflict and compromise between these two trends* . . . both kinds of instincts would be active in every particle of living substance, though in unequal proportions, so that some one substance might be the principle representative of Eros. This hypothesis throws no light whatever upon the manner in which the two classes of instincts are fused, blended, and alloyed with each other; but that this takes place regularly and very extensively is an assumption indispensable to our conception.[6] (Freud, 1923, pp. 40–1: my italics)

In this chapter Freud is at pains to distinguish the life from the death drive because they tend to get confused with each other. This blending would account for the confusion. But Freud also states that both instincts are working towards the original state of things that was disturbed by the emergence of life. The paradox here is that life was disturbed by the emergence of life. But it is in this confused passage that the evidence comes to the fore that life and Eros are not the same; that is, that Eros has this binding function ('so that some one substance might be the principle representative of Eros') but life has not: it shares its aim with death. The rescuing activity is exercised not by Eros but by the ego, which desexualizes libido. Finally, 'the Ego, by sublimating some of the libido for itself and its purposes, assists the id in its work of mastering the tensions' (ibid., p. 47). And Freud goes on by pointing out that it is the ego, on which Eros tries to exercise its binding function, which is the agency which desexualizes and sublimates this otherwise fatal Nirvana and its consuming 'enjoying' activity. This is the redeeming function of love I mentioned earlier, the function which is on the side of the ego-image. Love is desexualized libido. It saves your life.

I wrote 'enjoying', and not pleasurable, as Freud himself says that the pleasure principle does not apply to the life and death drives but to the ego. We can use the word 'enjoyment' to describe precisely this 'beyond pleasure' which Nirvana entails for both Eros and Thanatos. Where is this incomprehensible enjoying flow of life going? Nowhere else, Freud concludes, than towards death. In this way Eros comes to the service of the death drive, as a pleasurable, rather than enjoying tension; a suspension/friction acting on the homeostatic state. From this perspective life appears to act as a brake in the run towards its own exhaustion or sexual saturation. Humans can never let themselves enjoy life entirely if not at risk of death. There is an aspect of Eros which takes its time in preparing a scene, a framework within which enjoyment takes its time before running towards its own complete exhaustion, to death. It both postpones and gives access to a state which is careless about going on living,[7] about eternity or wisdom; it *wants to live all at once*.

This is that side of Eros which the ego aims either to domesticate or to split off from the official image we have of ourselves; as Eros includes also this not social but rather scandalous side, the one which has no aim and no ethics, it does not obey the edicts of language or the fascination of our image. It enjoys nothingness, runs towards the dissolution of our human boundaries, exceeds them, overflowing uncohesively towards an absolute, which we can reach, if only in the imagination, in death. We can see the death drive operating within Eros itself, and it is at this point that Freud shifts his earlier dualism between ego and sexual drives into a life–death dualism. In other words, both ego and Eros participate in life and death, as they are two different moments of the same tension. Every dualism hides a fusion, an intolerable sameness, a vicious circle. Dams have to be erected against the fatal flow of life, just as Freud spoke of the dams against libido.

It seems that, in order to survive, humans have to make a detour from life itself. They have to find another abode to keep a distance from their excess of life; a bit of death has to be introduced to keep life going. This cut into the enjoyment of life is called, in analytical terms, castration. This very castration, which we dread more than death, and which the neurotic takes for death, has the function of warding off death. Castration, by limiting life's brute activity, leaves a gap, which it will be up to language to fill and smooth away by giving it a meaning, by symbolizing it, and in a way by killing it. The name is the murder of the thing. Language, therefore, can include the erotic death drive only through a change of discourse; that is, by transforming it, the erotic thing, into a discourse of love. Love is then a desire to accomplish what Eros cannot accomplish: a unity, a continuity of the fusion with the desired object – love wants to fill the gaps of life left by Eros.

Therefore Eros and love are not the same thing, or rather they stand in two different positions in relation to their common 'content' – what we designated as x. This content or essence of Eros seems to coincide with a defect in the essence of life, with a negative agent and, therefore, with the inexpressible, which we have linked to death. Eros and love are not, then, the x but its effects, or rather its possibilities of expression and representation. Eros, while representing the drive which strives for homeostasis, provokes a tension that upsets and splits it, makes of a static state a wanting state. But love turns around an x, or rather evokes it. Love performs its evocatory rites, it enacts the lover's Dionysiac discourse. Love-making, for example, is a performance, it enacts love as the possibility of a fusion of two individuals in One: the possibility, indeed, of Nirvana. For Freud, Eros was the cohesive force of life whose goals are fusion and unity in opposition to the dividing and destructive death drive. Nevertheless, although love-making is the *mise-en-scène* of a desired union, it is not *it*. However much and satisfactorily two people copulate together, they will remain two, irreducibly separate and in conflict. What holds the two together is precisely love, which they enact in sexual or erotic activity. What holds them together is a desire to be once more one, and this is not achieved by the sexual act.

Hence love is this desire to be one but it is not one; all it can manage is to devise ways to achieve more permanent relations with the other, but it cannot escape from the fact that human beings are dramatically separate from each other and split within themselves by irreconcilable forces. Is love, then, an illusion or a utopia? There is love, we cannot deny that human beings love, that they strive towards the other, that they desire the other so long as they are human, that is, incomplete and lacking something. We desire . . . by loving. But if love finds a *love*-object, an image in which to stop the consuming activity of enjoyment, what about the *erotic* object? Does it coincide with the love-object? The problem is that Eros as a pure activity (force) keeps going; that is, it exists as long as it is deprived of its object. Lacan went so far as to say that love is loving what the other does not have and giving nothing in order not to deceive the other. This nothing is exactly the object of desire, the lack which causes its existence. This nothing is the object of the Freudian Eros.

But this nothing found a representation in Lacan, a little one, a little object (a) (*objet petit* (a)). However small a nothing this little thing might be, it will be hunted, and this hunting constitutes the essence of love; that is, the x which, unlike the Lacanian little (a), is desire itself. Whether by the analyst of texts or of minds, or by Swann's interpretative jealousy,[8] or by any of us in our daily dealings with signs, gestures, letters, poems, declarations, tears of love, this little (a) is hunted, read, interpreted, questioned, loved and hated, in an attempt to track it down in some way or other. All we can talk about when we talk about love is, therefore, this tracking down, this attempt to speak its enigma: a discourse on love indeed.

'There is no sexual rapport' as Lacan expressed it (1975, pp. 72–3). This means that there is no fusion or permanent union with the other, because a piece always goes missing. There is love so long as we continue to long for the missing piece, even after we happen (it does not always happen) to enjoy the other; in fact the discourse of love does not speak of enjoyment but of a 'driving factor'. I quote Freud: 'and it is the difference in amount between the pleasure of satisfaction which is *demanded* and that which is actually *achieved* that provides *the driving factor* which will permit of no halting at any position attained, but, in the poet's words, *ungebandigt immer vorwarts dringt* (Presses ever forward unsubdued)' (1920a, p. 42: Freud's italics and my underlines). This driving factor is what Lacan translated into the concept of desire; this is the *x* of love.

Platonic love

Let us examine now some aspects of love relating to the enjoyment of the erotic performance. Let us start from the most chaste form of love, platonic love, and let us quote what Socrates says in Plato's *Symposium*. This Platonic dialogue takes place at a banquet among some of the most illustrious Athenians of Socrates' time. They all agree on that occasion, apart from Alcibiades who arrives late, to refrain from drinking too much and to deliver in turn a speech on love. At his turn Socrates presents love as the son of Poverty and Contrivance:

> having Contrivance for his father and Poverty for his mother, he bears the following character. He is always poor, and, far from being sensitive and beautiful, as most people imagine, he is hard and weather-beaten, shoeless and homeless, always sleeping out for want of a bed, on the ground, on door-steps, and in the street. So far he takes after his mother and lives in want. But, being also his father's son, he schemes to get for himself whatever is beautiful and good; he is bold and forward and strenuous, always devising tricks like a cunning huntsman; he yearns after knowledge and is full of resource and is a lover of wisdom all his life, a skilful magician, an alchemist, a true sophist. *He is neither mortal nor immortal; but on one and the same day he will live and flourish (when things go well with him), and also meet his death; and then come to life again through the vigour that he inherits from his father.* What he wins he always loses, and is neither rich nor poor, neither wise nor ignorant. (Plato, 1951, p. 82: my italics)

Do we ever extinguish our demand for love, which started with our first wail, the moment we separated from the mother's body? We can see love born with life, out of its misery and out of its resources at the same time. It shares with life its poverty and its resources.

At a certain point, towards the end of the sober Socratic banquet devoted to love, Eros breaks in through the person of the handsome, rich and illustrious Alcibiades, who is drunk and in love. Alcibiades makes his own speech about Socrates himself, describing his own frustration at having failed to seduce him; how from being the most admired and loved man in Athens he became, after having met Socrates' great mind, a helpless lover; the more Socrates ignored his sexual approaches the more he felt ashamed of himself, poor, reverent towards Socrates' courageous character, and slavishly in love with him. But it is not with Socrates that Alcibiades is now in love but Agathon, the handsome tragic poet who is the host of the banquet and who is in his turn in love with Pausanias. The chain of love could continue endlessly, but it is to Socrates that Alcibiades addresses his discourse of love. This phenomenon is not far from what happens in the banquet of the analytical situation, where the subject discovers his lack by loving. But it is not with Socrates that the chain stops; on the contrary, he starts it off. Alcibiades' frustrated love for Socrates sets him to love beyond Socrates. It is the very fact that the analyst eludes the function of the desired object, precisely like Socrates, and does not fulfil the analysand's demand for love, that makes the analysand realize his/her want of love. It is the proper character of love not being concerned with the enjoyment one might get from it but, on the contrary, being devoid of any possession to enjoy, love is left with the lack of enjoyment. We could say that love intervenes imaginarily at the point when enjoyment must end: namely, when castration intervenes.

Could we say, then, that love is a mere illusion, imaginary, a phantasy? Eros is imaginary, it is the staging of an encounter with the object which always eludes our grasp, it gives a pleasure where an encounter with the enjoyment of the little (a) could have been. The erotic encounter gives a formal consistency to (a): the body and face of the loved other. We inhabit a world of images which gives us a human field of vision,[9] as we could not survive under the sway of the unseeing death drive which, as we have seen earlier, is the drive to consume life, to live all at once. But the relation of the (a) to an image is a double-edged one because, if illusions are vital in getting us to hover above the emptiness and terror that life affords us, erotic enjoyment without the 'sign' of love would plunge us into a devouring, nonsensical erotic passion for the other, where the borders of the image of her/his body would get consumed by a permanent enjoyment. A striking example of this consummation of the body is the Japanese film *Ai No Corrida*, where the two characters make love to each other in an augmentation of orgasmic enjoyment which gets closer and closer to total suffocation, the death of the male partner, and his mutilation, and ends with the female partner roaming a boundless place holding her partner's testicles.[10]

Sexual enjoyment

So, if sexual enjoyment is an enacting of our relation to (a) but is not it, love is the 'sign' which changes the discourse; it is a discourse on sexuality but is not sexuality. The commandment: 'Respect your father and your mother, so that you may live a long time in the land that I am giving you' commands respect,[11] that is, a distance from the loved object, which Freud formulated with the Oedipal prohibition in terms of 'love your parents but do not make love to them if you want to be an inhabitant of the earth.' Respect is love as social bonding; it is a renunciation of the enjoyment/consummation of the other's body[12] in order to be symbolically bound to the others. The banquet is the convivium of a chain of disappointed lovers. They can all sit at the same table.

However, if an absolute enjoyment is forbidden, we can, nevertheless, come near to it, experience it in particular situations, but only at the cost of not saying what it is. If you try to reveal it, you are already at an indecent banquet, like the drunken Alcibiades, and not part of the symposium of sober men.

The sexed body is indecent because it reveals itself not as a whole but as an unwhole, holed body. Sexuality is this fissure which breaks up the imaginary wholeness of the desired body. Mammary ducts, swelling of blood vessels, the lubricated vagina are the islands of *jouissance*, the canals and bridges leading into erotic experience. But it does not last, there is no eternal sexual intercourse but scansions, glitterings and fadings of the possession of the object. The body functions, then, as a point of passage between the envelope of the human image and its violation. It contains the seducing trace of its own limit, it opens onto the limitlessness of *jouissance*.[13]

Often art makes attempts to reveal something of this *a*. Literature, cinema, theatre have tried and go on trying to show and catch Eros in the open act. George Bataille (1988) makes us plunge into the crude erotic matter in a world of uncanny images and perversions. The crudeness of the erotic act breaks through the fictional images to re-establish the priority of the 'real' itself in the look of the spectator, who is cajoled into taking an active role, as when Mme Edwarda, in the novel of the same name, hypnotizes the baffled visitor with a raw exhibitionism which culminates in her words, 'Look, this is God.' Or, as in another of George Bataille's novels, *Ma Mère*, the protagonist, in casually coming across old porno-pictures, experiences and discovers his mother's vocation as a vestal of Eros. Art welcomes the erotic representation, its perturbations and excitement, into its fictions. But it is not a simple erotic *mise-en-scène* to amuse the senses (one cannot say this of Sade or of Bataille); rather the body is there to be either violated or redeemed. Art's discourse of love is a discourse of its own, with its own relations to its own object.

Most of Buñuel's film images – a woman greedily enraptured by sucking the foot of a statue, or a cow walking into a bedroom as if it were in its own stable – that refer to this enjoyment are of an uncanny effect, caught into the fiction and threatening its weave and structure. It was characteristic of surrealism to take on the erotic danger as its own challenge to language, its own way to say what cannot be said.

Erica Jong, in her novel *Fear of Flying* (1974) appears very determined to beat her fist against the wall that language has built around feminine sexuality. She tries hard to confess her enjoyment, whereas all she can do is to describe, through its failures, her search for it. And, in the end, in her *How to Save Your Own Life* (1977), it is love which comes out triumphant. When she has come to terms with the limitations of Eros and the impossibility of enjoying it fully, her novel ends with love poems. Jong fails the enjoyment of her Icarian flight into sex and, in so doing, saves her life by a hair's breadth, by a change of literary discourse. Poetry is the realm of love. The troubadours enjoyed singing their love to their quasi-unattainable ladies. Love and language are related, they are both deferment and desire. We could say that if sexual intercourse can produce new human life, love, in its intercourse with language, produces inspiration.

Mystical love

But one might still wonder whether there could be some other way to reveal this clandestine enjoyment. Lacan pointed out one category of lovers who can talk unashamedly about it, though very rarely. These are those mystics who experience the ecstasy of their encounters with God: what we could literally call the enjoyment of God. The concept of God, whether God is feared or disbelieved in, functions as the signifier of the absolute. It is the name by which language designates its border with what lies beyond itself, God as its creator, the Word itself, the *Verbum*. So the enjoyment of God as absolute enjoyment is the final aim of man's love, as was pointed out by the prostitute Mme Edwarda. But the mystics, who experience it, cannot usually speak about it; they just experience it. Some people, such as the thirteenth-century Sufi poet Rumi and the Christian northern mystic Hadewijch d'Anvers,[14] have borne witness licitly, without shame, in poetry, in the language of love again. Hadewijch d'Anvers describes it thus:

> I languish, I attend, I relish
> the God which fills me with sweetness;
> I know, I feel and I find
> recompense for my sufferings.
>
> I suffer, I strive, I stretch beyond myself,
> I feed with my blood (this God who was born inside myself);
> I hail the divine Sweetness
> which recompensates the fury of love. (1985, MGD. XV)
> (Translated into English by the author)

Hadewijch conceives of an escalation from love, which is renunciation, mortification and pain, towards an absolute ecstatic enjoyment.[15] The mystical practice realizes what the mystery rites introduce us to. Etymologically the word 'mystic' springs from the Greek μυστηριον, mystery. In the Greek Dionysiac rites the mystical experience is supposed to follow the accomplishment of the unveiling, and a consequent unveiling of the souls of the initiates, but what all this was an initiation into remains indeed the mystery. But in Pompeii we are left with images which represent figuratively what Hadewijch describes in writing. It seems paradoxical that Christian mystics are able to say, even though only from the border of heavy veils, what pagan cults could not say, but left as mysteries. In the transposition of Greek gods into Latin culture they lose the mysteric dimension. Instead, it is ascribed to a minor god like

Bacchus, who, paradoxically, is the most earthly and sensual god. Latin religion is not mystical. We had to wait for Christianity to reappropriate and give priority to the mystical aspect of the mysteries. This mystical emphasis can be explained by the passage from pagan polytheism to Christian monotheism. The Greek gods did not allow the possibility of a relation with the One; in other words, did not allow an articulation as radical as that of the Christian fusion and Oneness with God.[16] Hadewijch dares to articulate even though, and even when, words fail her at the apex of her revelations: 'In the intimacy of the One, these souls are pure and naked inwardly, without images, without figures, as if freed from time, uncreated, released from their limits in the silent latitude. And here I stop, no longer finding either end nor beginning, *nor comparison which may justify the words*' (1985, p. 45: my italics).

So divine love cannot be justified by Greek culture, if not as a secret for the few, and seems to contain an obscenity impossible to divulge. The Romans tamed this obscenity, as do family planning clinics, by venerating the god of power, the Phallus. If the particular eroticism which is represented in the Villa of the Mysteries as an enjoying god is more perturbing sexually than religiously, this may be because pagan gods were *not* gods of love, or rather, their discourse is not a discourse of absolute love, whose discourse is the only one which justifies this enjoyment beyond words. Also Hadewijch traces out a path of mysteric undressing which allows her to map the altitudes of experience. The apex of her experience is on 'a bare and harsh desert'. But it is in this desert, in this absence of images, veils of the soul, that presence becomes possible. The mystical path starts with this presence of an absence, it equals an 'external sensation'. The two lovers look for, intermingle and feel each other. It is an encounter of two who aim at a fusion, at becoming One. This is ecstasis, a revelation 'which cannot be, the pure and naked Nothing' (Hadewijch d'Anvers, 1985, p. 45). 'After this I remained united to my lover to the point of blending entirely in him so that *nothing* was left of me' (van Mierlo, 1924: my italics).

Reaching the One is also a total loss of oneself – one ceases to think of or imagine oneself at all – as well as a revelation which cannot be revealed if not to 'uncreated' souls: the One is a return to an original state before separation, that is, before one's creation. Here we have Nirvana as our end and our beginning. The mystical bet is that only God can allow one to refind this place, but only if one follows a particular path. This was related to Socrates by Diotima in terms of a progression according to which even the most inferior form of love, heterosexuality, is already potentially love of God. It is precisely this goal-directed progression of love, which Hadewijch, like Diotima, describes, that differentiates the mystical philosophical experience from the delusional experience described by psychotic people. In both cases, mystical and psychotic, we have an experience of enjoyment of God and the necessity to write about it, as in the case of President Schreber's 'Memoirs' (Freud, 1911), to find a communicable coherence for an experience which cannot be integrated into ordinary knowledge. But whereas the mystic welcomes this experience, the psychotic is forced into a submission to it. The one accepts losing her/his own subjectivity because it remains guaranteed, inscribed in a framework, the religious one, which justifies and allows its accomplishment. The other has not subjectivized it: Schreber does not love – or even believe in – this God, whose voluptuousness he does not doubt, though. He only experiences the external sensations, without a desired or sought-after lover.

This is the psychotic, senseless certainty where the delusion lies outside the subject as an objective fact, resistant to any integration into the world of the subject. In fact, according to Freud, the formation of a delusional system is an attempt at self-cure, an attempt to integrate this 'real', unwanted experience of voluptuousness into a system. Schreber has to make up a theological system to justify it. Hadewijch, too, writes about her experience, also a voluptuous one, but one for which her spiritual choice had made her prepared. In her progressive unveiling she has also offered her flesh to God in torments and a 'fury' of love which are her voluntary payment and her debt for her ecstasy. Ecstasy is the result of a path or of an accepted call. It is different from the Wolf-man's hallucination of the cut finger, which took him by surprise and sank him into a timeless immobility and terrified muteness. Schreber's memoirs are an attempt to accept his hallucinations by turning them into an odd divine call and, therefore, to show the German law court that he was not insane, that his experience was not senseless. Hadewijch legitimized her experience within the Catholic church instead.

Language allows the enjoyment of God only if love is entailed in the subject's progression, if a sacrifice is chosen in order to enjoy.

Schreber's howling preceded a humiliating, shameful voluptuousness. A search for God preceded Hadewijch's mystical encounters. Love tends towards God, who is the signifier of the total wholeness unveiled, of the void. Only with Him would love and enjoyment finally coincide. He is the limit between language and *jouissance*, and after Him we seek our lost unity, which would coincide with Eros at last.

This phenomenology of the mystical encounter is important for Lacan, not because, as is sometimes vulgarly believed, mystics get a sexual enjoyment from their hysterical relation to God, but for the opposite reason – because sexual enjoyment is a faint reproduction of divine ecstasy, in the way in which young boys were for Diotima a faint image of absolute beauty. And it is this disjunction between sex and what transcends it in its enjoyment that constitutes the typically Lacanian problematic of feminine sexuality. It is this other enjoyment, which is the one of the woman, still enigmatic and ineffable, which might partake of the paradigm of the mystical experience; a participation which also constitutes the watershed between divine and profane love. The question of such a watershed is served in an interesting way at the banquet where feminism and Lacan have invited themselves to deliver their speech, or really their question, concerning the woman's enjoyment. To Lacan's (and Freud's) question: 'What does she want?' feminists answer, 'If this is our lot – to choose to subject ourselves to him for a bit of enjoyment – thank you, we don't want it.' And Lacan could answer, 'Yes, you don't want it because you are women and not The Woman (who does not exist).[17] But if The Woman existed she would want exactly that (and mystics and saints are people who have placed themselves in a purely feminine position *vis-à-vis* God).'

Undoubtedly some women can achieve their sexual enjoyment only if they identify their man partner with a godlike figure, as if they can allow themselves some enjoyment from the other's body only if it can be transcended. A woman such as this expects from the man more than sex; she expects love as the condition of enjoying him. She, like the mystic, can abandon herself to him and have her enjoyment justified by his and her love. Many women in order to enjoy must love, and in that case, like the mystics, they admit their enjoyment unashamedly. For men this mystical enjoyment is more difficult; as they desire to represent God for women, they aim at a different enjoyment, which is tied up with the laws of language.

They enjoy being the divine word represented by the law and authority of the phallus. God is male in Western mysticism.

The phallus is a pagan idol too, and its cult flourished in Roman culture to the detriment of eastern Dionysiac rites. Its symbol is carved on the walls of the commercial high road in Pompeii, as a symbol of wealth, fertility and potency. It is part of the cult of the *agora*, the public square. Men identify with its power, with this simulacrum, this earthly representation of God. But in so doing they miss precisely that *jouissance* that some women obtain by renouncing the unspoken wish to be God and, therefore, by enjoying Him in him; whereas men, if they have to represent godly mastery in relation to women, cannot enjoy God, cannot enjoy divinely. From this position men's sexual enjoyment does not aim at oneness, but returns on their own body and, more precisely, on their organ. They enjoy their own organ under the auspices of the idol Phallus. Masculine desire turns around an imaginary mastery and sexual potency which are the phallus's requirements. No wonder then if what men dread most and suffer mostly from is sexual impotence, as the potency the phallus requires from men is an unsustainable one. In fact it breaks down in front of the paradoxical task of having to represent the law which banishes sexuality and having to use their penis to make women enjoy that law. That is why so often women and their bodies have represented and still represent sexual indecency and tempting evil; their lack of a penis is in a blatant conflict with man's phallic desire. That might explain also why homosexuality, however formally condemned by most societies, has always been men's obvious tendency.

In the *Symposium* it is the common opinion that heterosexual love is men's lowest kind of love and that only homosexuality is dignified and, therefore, truly enjoyable. The woman, in order to be desired, has to be erected to turn herself into the phallus of men. This will be 'courtly love's' role.

Courtly love

The cult of women started much later in our culture, with the troubadours' love songs and courtly love. The woman, debased and mortified by Christianity as the representative of sexuality, was now desired, but at a due distance. Desire augmented with her absence. Temptations were allowed so long as they titillated the senses enough to keep desire from drying up. Courtly love functions as a sort of domestication of desire; marriage would, in fact, have stopped this courtesy of love. Divinity here becomes Woman (the reverse of the mystic) and, therefore, she becomes idol.

The only way men can enjoy women's bodies is, then, to elevate them to the status of an idol, to phallicize them: woman's body can be desired as the veil which hides the phallus; she has, then, to be desexualized and idealized in order to be desired. But it happens to men that under a woman's veil or dress they enjoy – surprise – a vagina instead of a penis, and that can be a nice surprise for some, but horror and ill-concealed disgust for others. The example of Tristan and Isolda illustrates well the dread of martyrdom that letting oneself go into the abyss of heterosexual love entails. It equals letting oneself go into the claws of the death drive. Eros is still for courtly lovers, as it is for the Catholic church, linked to death of the spirit.

The great mystics could attain their spiritual union with God by suffering a letting go of their own flesh, going through the claws of bodily pleasures and torments which the lover lavishes on the partner. These mystics are frequently women, not because of their biology, but because they occupy a purely feminine position *vis-à-vis* God's love. Courtly love claims Eros back into the world by claiming the woman back from God for man. Man's love for her certainly emancipates her from Christian mortification, gives her an imaginary freedom and elevation, so long as it avoids erotic consummation. The courtly man claims back the woman but not the Eros which goes with her. The woman as real fascinates but terrifies too. The masculine response to this terror, apart from homosexuality, can be lust and perversion, a humiliating or sinful enjoyment. The forbidden mother's body remains forbidden by father.

A *phallic jouissance* is offered in the place of the (a) which women represent. These two absolute positions, whether one pretends to exist (phallic) or not exist (Woman), seem to be incompatible. Their enjoyments skim over each other only by an impure encounter of the sexes, somewhere half-way between phallic and the *Other* (feminine) *jouissance*. For a man occupying the masculine place in the intercourse succeeds in enjoying like a woman only if he gives up representing mastery and potency, as well as renouncing the myth of the genital orgasm as the only enjoyment (like Dionysus in plate 5). And a woman, unlike Edwarda and the woman in *Ai No Corrida*, enjoys only if she gives up exhibiting and opening herself to the devouring void of annihilation. There is no sexual rapport, says Lacan, but there is Eros, which is sexual relation, attempts at an exchange, a transport for the other. But were this other reached, s/he would disappear as other. The ecstatic moment is the transcendence of any difference, of indeed the sexual one. We could call it, in analytical terms, the transcendence of the phallus.

The initiates of Tantra, whose erotic rites are based on the suspension of ejaculation to obtain a sense of endless ecstasy, enjoy their eroticism as suspension and delay in opposition to the orgasmic conception of western sexuality. Eros is a necessary detour, a rite which only strives for an ascesis in mystical love, where the function of Eros is a project for *jouissance* that has been truly earned (the payment of the debt with castration). The aim of eastern eroticism is to throw a shadow over both the all-powerful man and the all-lacking woman; that is, over the phallic difference. It is an attempt at the partners enjoying in equality. Western culture's 'sexual liberation' failed as an attempt to equalize *jouissance in differentia*. From the Greeks up to the gay movement, homosexuality claims and exalts the project of an erotica. Homosexuality seems to promise what a heterosexual erotica failed to achieve: to transcend the obstacles of difference, the abyss of the other. But, whether homo or hetero, the love relation is always addressed to a third which transcends the two, who would be otherwise incompatible, and which makes their relation an endeavour beyond themselves. The partners, like two pagan priests, are to evoke the phallus hidden behind the veil of shame (plate 6) and, hopefully, God willing, enjoy it *in absentia*.

2

What is the Psychoanalyst Supposed to Know?

Pompeii is my metaphor. Perhaps it is only by writing to the reader as an analysand that I can transmit something as an analyst: metaphors, images, experiences to which the reader can give a meaning, in the same way that our analysands convey a meaning to us just by speaking themselves. No person transmitted psychoanalytical knowledge to its inventor except those women who lay on his couch one by one, as our analysands lie on our couches one by one with their single, unrepeatable and unique histories and little stories. I find it difficult to think how psychoanalysis could be transmitted otherwise. The transmission of psychoanalysis is a rite of love, but love is always a quest for knowledge. We seem to need another to give our message back to us, because we do not know what it is.

We go to the analyst in order to know what it is that we are saying and cannot recognize but whose effects make themselves painfully felt. Or better, something suffers in us through the symptom, be it mere unhappiness. So we go to psychoanalysts assuming that they know what this symptom is about; we assume they know the truth about us. But the poor analysands will soon lose their illusions and realize that the whole trick in psychoanalysis is that you have to find the truth for yourself. What is, therefore, this truth one finds just by speaking oneself? What is this claim? Of course a search for truth has always animated humankind. Even dictators and slaves claim a truth.

So, what is so special about the analytical couple in its search for truth? Nothing other than the discovery that truth is relative, partial and personal, that truth flashes through lies, that it never makes itself manifest in its wholeness. We could say that the logical paradox of the claim 'I am lying' represents the analytical truth. No one can claim absolute truth. But there is no such thing as an absolute lie either, precisely because it is through lies that truth peeps out, just as the sun does through the thick foliage of a tree. But as with the sun, one cannot look at it directly, because, like Oedipus in the face of the truth of his parricide and incest, one would be blinded by it. Just as we can look at the sun sparkling through the gaps in the foliage, so we can see some truth through the holes of our discourse: a slip of the tongue, the absurdity of a dream, a haunting oblivion.

However absurd it might seem, truth and knowledge are irreconcilable and we are split between them. Truth is exiled from our knowing ego. The apparently paradoxical task psychoanalysis has to accomplish is to find again something which we had originally refused to acknowledge, but which nevertheless strives for acknowledgement. Such an acknowledgement is very difficult, precisely because we 'want to be' through the wholeness of our egos which, by definition, cannot acknowledge any split, except by repressing it. What we have to recognize, therefore, is this very split, this cut – like a hole – in the centre of our being.

In this way truth presents itself to us at the borders of our assumed being, as non-being, as what does not make sense, a nonsense. In this negative and ungraspable form it presents itself as a stranger to our assumed existence; it evokes death. This non-being is to the analyst the truth of our being, which we cannot accept. It comes out in the psychoanalytical discourse as a part cut off from us, barring us and making of us split beings. For Lacan, the subject is always a barred or split subject. Our language cannot express what is left over from the ego's apprehension of its wholeness if not as an interruption, a logical contradiction, a discord in our conscious and ethical thought, and at its worst – as in neurosis – as a symptom. In our practice we come up against an ethical problem concerning our very being: we come very close to the ethical problem that 'being' constituted for Hamlet. Whereas we take up being, though in a negative form, through pain, denials and lies, it – nonbeing – speaks through us. This is the language of the unconscious, of the holes in our discourse. Psychoanalysis can allow holes to speak, and the unconscious is their language.

The psychoanalyst listens, then, to a discourse on the frontier of the analysand's very being. Here we are, placed on the edge of a precipice which we cannot ignore and which, hopefully, we will not fall into. I say hopefully, for at the end of the psychoanalytical process we should find ourselves at the right distance from our being. As analysts and analysands, we sometimes go too far one way or the other: we run desperately after unconscious ghosts and primordial feelings to fill the gap we are faced with, or we reinforce models of social integration and our conscious clichés of well-being.

Whatever model we follow as analysts, our discourse comes to a halt in front of the unspeakable dimension of death and sexual enjoyment, witnessed by the silence which marks their entry; something comparable to what the mystics experience but cannot speak about. Wanting to know or say more would endanger their innocence *vis-à-vis* God. Our conscious knowledge is the fig leaf that covers our original nakedness. It seems that all human knowledge is built on this ignorance of our original state, by means of an original repression. The analytical unconscious deals precisely with this loss of innocence, that is, with its acknowledgement (shame).[1] The analysand ends up in our consulting rooms haunted by the images which come to crowd in an absence. To encounter an absence: something is missing. This entails our yearning, grieving and desiring something.

But what is this something which we seem to be after but which we avoid like the plague? Neither analysand nor analyst is supposed to know it because the object of our desire is exactly the thing that is missing. Or more precisely, we desire it because of its very lack. We desire it exactly because we have not got it. Desire is desire for what we have irremediably lost, for what we refuse stubbornly to desire and yet still desire. With psychotics, instead, we are plunged into the senseless presence of that which has been radically rejected.[2] They bear witness to a radical state of being thrown into the world. In their case and in the case of neurotics, in different ways, the original repression has not found a representation by which it can be recognized and dealt with.

This problem was well illustrated by Lacan's pupil Lefort in a case of a four-year-old boy,[3] called by her the 'wolf-child'. This boy, besides howling and whirling desperately all over the place most of the time, could say only two words, one of which was 'wolf'. Moreover, it was thanks to this word that the boy could represent and communicate his state of being plunged into a sort of animal world, wild and dangerous. By naming this animal he represented himself as an animal, but so long as he could speak and represent himself, he was human. This word, then, as the core of language for this boy, was a bridge with a human world; he could communicate to others his state and what he was: actually a wolf, though potentially a child. And as a child, at the end of the therapy, he could play at being a wolf without being one.

If a child does not play, it is bad news; we would all agree that the child is disturbed. Winnicott used his first sessions with young children and mothers to test their capacity to play, before he worked out what was wrong between them. Playing entails a split in the players, between themselves and the representation of themselves. When playing chess, players are distinct from the pawn on the chessboard and they will not be personally in danger when their king is in check. But the king is representing the player, it is standing in the place of a subject who is partly absent from the game: partly there and partly not there, present and absent, split in a multiplicity of levels of existence.

Freud realized, when observing his little grandchild playing at 'gone' and 'back' with the cotton reel at the end of the thread while the child's mother was away, that, by representing the absence of his mother in his play and in his words, the child was trying to master that absence and make it bearable. Certainly an actor and a musician exist beyond their playing, but their playing is their expression, they are in it. What would an artist be without painting or writing, or even myself were I unable to speak of my unbearable earthquakes? In writing to the reader I can evoke the precariousness of my enjoyable, faraway land. Words open for us a world pregnant with images, possibilities and meaning.[4] Speaking and writing are play, but by them we also assume our division between different levels of existence, between presence and absence, life and death, transience and permanence; between me and the other, between me and you. Speaking contains already all the polyvalence of our status as human beings.

Yet there is nothing we tolerate worse than the freedom to speak. Freud showed how, through the power of hypnosis, the therapist found very little resistance, and the hysterical symptoms seemed promptly relieved by the hypnotic transference. But when Freud asked Dora to speak freely, without hypnosis, she put up the most stubborn resistance. And so analysts too may consider finding the same freedom intolerable.

Freedom to speak is what in analytical terms is called 'free association'. In effect, this is a phenomenon where we lose mastery of our speech; in freedom we are subjected to uncontrolled thoughts and words; they speak through us as if we were spoken rather than speaking. In the freedom of speech we come to realize our subjection to speech itself. This is the psychoanalytical unconscious; to speak freely means to let the unconscious speak. This is what we require from our analysands, and from ourselves.

Can one imagine that Freud could have come anywhere near the discovery of the unconscious if he had followed the path that the medical training and ethics of his times demanded from him? Freud *discovered* his way to *invent*. An invention is not caused by a magical power, but by finding again what had been lost, discarded and forgotten, or repressed by everybody else. That is what Freud did in order to make himself a psychoanalyst. Refusing to use his medical knowledge or hypnotic suggestion, Freud risked his professional standing but set free his desire to understand and then invent.

But today it seems as if we are not yet able to devise a professional transmission outside the models of army or church, or even the pathogenic family. Psychoanalysts, as much as colonels and priests, fear being deviant in how they 'do' psychoanalysis.

As Moustafa Safouan stresses in his book on the formation of analysts (1983),[5] for Freud the social order has its roots in the murder of the father. As long as the primitive father ruled, however enlightened and generous we want to believe he was, the horde had no law but the arbitrary authority of a father who was the sole possessor of all chattels, all women and all power. The father of the law rises from this dead tyrant. The symbolic father is the giver of the law, a gift of possible fairness.

Only by murder could the sons come to terms with their authentic human limits and insufficiency. For Freud, the original impotence of human beings is the first source of all moral motivations. That means that as long as the wild figure of the all-powerful father persists in our unconscious, even when masked by the good analyst and supervisor with uncontested power of judgement and knowledge, we can only desire his death, because we are dispossessed of our own judgement and knowledge.

Hegel was not far from this when he devised the impasse of the master–slave couple, where the slave accepts being a slave to save his life, only so that he can keep the typically neurotic procrastinating certainty that one day his master will die and he himself be free. The slave can then procrastinate: he can wait and wait, for the master to die.

So, with the death of the father the sons can make the law and authorize somebody to represent it. The law, even when dictated by a tyrant, is different from the arbitrary power of the primal father. Still, the law of the father haunts the neurotic, coming back as the father's ghost, as it did with Hamlet. This clinging to the law of a vengeful father serves the task of masking and hiding the sense of relativity and fragmentation of the world and of its no less incomprehensible laws. It serves the task of deferring our encounter with the ultimate law of death.

A lucid mind like Michel Foucault realized that, if one looks at the modern democratic state for the Marxian centre of power, one cannot find it in the close network of social and individual rules and disciplines. At the centre there is no power to conquer or to destroy, but only a meticulous control over people's behaviour, and a cultural conditioning springing from all points of the thick social network.

The law, whether democratic or tyrannical, always serves the task of warding off and replacing our uncontrollable ultimate masters: sex and death. Psychoanalysis aims instead at an encounter with our ultimate masters, and in order to make it possible it has to renounce all power, all illusory intermediaries between the subject and his/her nothingness. Analysis must give the subject the chance to meet his/her own void, the other form of his/her being which claims its rights (and rites). The analyst is often silent in order not to disturb the emergence of the subject's specific other which s/he came to settle accounts with. In order to do this, the analyst has to renounce professional authority and the power of knowledge, which the subject demands but must challenge.

The analytical challenge corresponds to the freeing of one's own desire to be and exist in spite of the awareness of death, which leads to a radical revision of the fixed meaning of our existence, to a world of new meanings. It does this once desire has been set free.

The analysis ends with the freeing of the analysand's desire to know. But there the analyst starts. Indeed, that would be quite enough for an analyst to start with – how not to know and, therefore, how to let the analysand find new representations in the crumbling ruins of his/her previous interpretations of the world. It is the revelation of an inadequate or partial meaning that demands a reconstitution from the ruins; it demands new building work, it demands the inventive creativity of the analytical work.

It is difficult to know why, but it is incontestable that the revelation of a previously disavowed meaning is the trick which cures a neurosis; the mind seems to be sick of lies. The job of the analyst is, then, not far from a Socratic maieutics, a midwifery that was meant to help deliver a truth which was emerging from the subject's speech. But, in addition, the analyst has to help deliver a subjective truth which emerges from the split and lack of being rather than from the imaginary wholeness and unity of our 'knowing' egos.

In the disintegration of all the ego's images, separation and mourning are unavoidable stages. After the death of the imaginary father, mourning takes the place of the euphoric whirls of relief and guilt. Once we have come to the realization that we lack the absolute father, our desire as analysts, which was kept repressed and indestructibly fixated on the father, might find itself freed, but only at the cost of finding ourselves separated, unglued. Not only have our analytical fathers and mothers, Freud, Klein or Lacan, died, but the imaginary father, the ghost which stages the phantom of the parricide *ad infinitum*, has to disappear.

Our identity as analysts cannot escape what no analysand can escape in the analytical process: a relationship full of perturbing truth, in the same way as the initiatory rites were the pathway to the otherwise terrifying unveiling. But the analyst is not supposed to know what is under the dark veil. No one knows what is hidden under the veil of the terrified woman (plate 4) who precedes the ecstasy of a god in this temple of love (plate 5).

The preparatory rites on one wall (plates 2 and 3), the impudent, human blissfulness of a god resting on a feminine lap in the middle (plate 5), the winged Demon of Shame lashing the penitent alongside a dancing figure (plates 6 and 7) and the girl's serene but ringed eyes reflected in a mirror on the other side (plate 8) illustrate the enigmatic and forbidden action of the unveiling itself, not what is unveiled. Visitors leave both perturbed and serene, as if they now knew something. The analyst might either give an idle interpretation or be like the visitor conducted in front of the enigmatic images of a dream. The analyst might look at these frescos and know something without knowing what it is. The analyst desires to know.

To know is the analyst's desire. They desire to know the truth because they know they do not have it. They are like the Domina (plate 1) of the villa who starts and directs the rites of the unveiling and gives access to the mysteries of our mind. The analytical room can well represent this villa, now even more mysterious, since all that is left are its veils, the representation of its rites but not the rites themselves. We can only interpret them, try to decipher their enigmatic representation. The analyst's desire is moved by this impossible revelation. Thus, he cannot help running after truth, even though, as with me in Pompeii, one has only left it at home.

3

The Passion of Childhood

An encounter with a Kleinian training was difficult and impassioned work, and by this I do not mean impassioning. It is not
the charm of its style that drags one into its net; it was, rather, that
one is bundled into a sack of all one's own infantile passions.

But let us not cry shame at this word 'passions', now out of use
and resistant to psychoanalytical assimilation. The word 'feelings'
seems to suit better both the Kleinians, and the British object-relations school in general, as it helps to give a neutral and neutered
connotation to their descriptions of wild and schizoid infantile
emotions and phantasmagorias. But from a Lacanian perspective,
passions do not fare that well either. Certainly they can be dusted
off as a 'pathos of the soul' or as 'passion of the signifier'. But the
mathematical (topological, as they are more usually known) formulations of Lacan are an attempt to remove the epic flesh of myths to
reveal the symbolic structure. They do this in contrast to psychoanalytical myths such as the true and false self, developmental stages,
'feelings' and so forth.

But if the Kleinian runs the risk of living in the cellar, in the dust
of archaic myths and feelings, could not the Lacanian too be
tempted to place passion back in the topological attic, to discuss it as
merely an imaginary relation to the world?

In order to avoid a position of 'belle âme', that is, in order to
avoid the risk of 'not wanting to know' anything about passion[1]
(whereas the object-relation analysts want to know them, as
'feelings', too much), I would like to examine the nature of the
theoretical contrast between the two clinical approaches mentioned
above.

First, I want to dwell a little on the gap that separates pathos (in the sense of Greek 'suffering' – pathology – and in the sense of Latin *passus, patior* – to be at the mercy of passion) and the world of topological and conceptual solutions. The analytical concept is not like the philosophical or mathematical one, the intrinsic product springing from its own conceptual logic. The analytical concept is an interpretation, and the interpretation is by definition one among many possible ones. The analytical interpretation, therefore, does not aim at the philosophical truth but at effects of truth over a spread of heterogeneous elements. After all, in spite of the right interpretation, the right guidelines, in spite of a good training, the analyst cannot avoid the long process of analysis.

Even though the good interpretation has immediate or automatic consequences, it is never the final solution. The process of analysis is itself this contrast of inhabiting an uncomfortable place, of hovering between mother earth and the skies of the father. That is the analysand's place as well as the analyst's. Here we are back at the problem of the gap, of the 'not knowing' discussed in the last chapter, which, unlike other disciplines, psychoanalysis should be in a position to acknowledge.

Is psychoanalysis a practice like the scientist's, the craftworker's, or even the cook's? And in what way is theory implicated in each of these practices? One possible answer to the second question is that all these practices base themselves on a *savoir faire*, 'knowing how to do', rather than on theoretical knowledge. A craftworker does not need to know the chemical formula of the material s/he is forging, although s/he knows the operations necessary to forge it, how to bend it, what gets lost in the process, what to curve and what to eliminate. In the applied sciences too the theoretical result is the product of experiments and errors from which a theory will be extracted *après coup*. As for the culinary recipe, even if the cook would like to reveal it, the results are as different as the infinite possibilities of culinary interpretations. Analysis too is a practice, but one from which a recipe is required. Artists do not have to and, often, do not want to answer for the process of their work either to themselves or to others. Analysts do. They cannot concede to themselves an answer like, 'Do your business, your pictures, your choice dishes, I'll do mine.' After all, their work consists precisely in doing the business of others, but in a very peculiar way, not in the way a gossip or confidante happens to deal with one's intimacy.

It is demanded of analysts to know the business of human beings. They are given the role of 'the one who is supposed to know' it already. As I suggested in the last chapter, we could say analysts are delegated to know our business not because they already know it, but in order to let them know our business which *we do not want to know*. The analyst is, therefore, the one supposed to want to know the business others do not want to know: a business, indeed, of desire. That is why, unlike the ancient prophets, the analyst does not pretend to know or to reveal a hidden truth. Unfortunately there is no revealed or revealable truth, not even for the analyst.

The problem is that if there were a revealed truth, if all truth could be revealed, there would no longer be any unconscious and analysts themselves would not need years and years of training, of analysis, of practice, almost initiation, in order to have just a glimpse of the bottomless abyss of the unconscious, as what, even after you have said everything, is still not said. That is why those who have attempted to describe it, to give it a form, a system, have left intact its mystery. That is why we go on questioning the analyst and why the analyst goes on questioning her/himself about the mystery of her/his knowledge. But that tells us also why the analyst is not *knowing* but rather doing, like the cook for example. Analysis is more like a *savoir faire*, a 'knowing how' to deal with a truth which never reveals itself for what it is; the analyst presupposes it but does not define it. In this respect, it is like the product of the artist which suffices to legitimate itself as such. For analysts also, the accomplishment of their work should suffice as its own legitimation. More often than not, analysts, seized by a desire for recognition, want their knowledge understood more in terms of the scientific authority of our culture than in terms of the validity of their product.

Unlike Kleinians with their internal world, or Jungians with their archetypal cosmology, or American psychologists who go hunting for the unconscious with the weapon of the ego, Lacan tries to stop wanting to define the unconscious; he defines only what it looks like, or rather, what it sounds like . . . it sounds like a language, where that which cannot be said speaks all the time, most often in vain. The analyst does not have the immediate word of revelation, which should not be surprising. Even the ancient augurs, or any revealed truth like the Bible or the oracle of Delphi (which, by telling Oedipus the truth, sends him in a direction which is the opposite to the advised one), have to be given an ear and then interpreted and often, as in the case of Oedipus, misinterpreted.

The imaginary in Klein and Lacan

When Lacan started to elaborate his own theory about the function of the ego, at the moment of his divergence from orthodox Freudians, his legitimate and respected interlocutor was Klein. He also engaged in a collegiate spirit with eminent analysts of the British school of object-relations such as Winnicott, Balint and Macalpine. In fact, it was by going over all the thematics of object-relations theory that Lacan came to organize his own particular vision; his focus shifted to the relation between the subject and the world. But in this relation, the question about the object remains a problematic moment. Such problematics influenced Lacan throughout his first period of theoretical elaboration concerning the imaginary order, and includes his theoretical efforts to locate a structure in which object-relation theory's dualism (between mother and infant) was a necessary moment but not a founding and isolated element.

The importance of the Kleinian contribution resides in having swept away the dichotomy between the real and imaginary status of the psychic object by installing the concept of 'psychic reality'. This reality contrasts with and is also analogous to Hegel's theory, when it affirms that what is imaginary (the Kleinian phantasy) is real, and that what is real is imaginary. Lacan was elaborating something quite similar to this in 1936 with *Beyond the Reality Principle* (1966a) and later in his 'Mirror stage' (1977d): the ego which governs the reality principle is of a purely imaginary nature. Such an idea is basic to his critique of scientific methodology (Benvenuto and Kennedy, 1986, ch. 3). And it is from this common Lacanian and Kleinian premise, this stress on the imaginary function, that I shall sketch the two different ways in which the question concerning the passions has developed.

Klein calls the organization of the patient's phantasmatic objects psychic or 'internal reality': a reality, therefore, which is both analogous to and in contrast with what is called 'external reality'. The Kleinian analytical process unfolds between these two realities by means of projection and introjection. It is through these mental mechanisms that the two realities both melt into each other and split from each other as if in a game of distorting mirrors, as they do between the baby and the breast, child and mother, analyst and analysand. The Kleinian attempt aims at apprehending a mental object by articulating the objects of the primordial infantile phantasies. The nature of this apprehension is not properly defined by Klein but it is described as the effect of mechanisms of interaction between internal and external.

The Kleinian object is an effect of *reinternalization*: the infant reclaims parts of a primordial object which it is gradually losing in the process of interaction with the real or external world. That is why the breast is for Kleinians the key object, what we could call the first signifier, in relation to which the surrounding world will take on its form and meaning. Hanna Segal (1986) has argued that the affects shift from the primordial objects towards new objects through equations, rather than symbols: *symbolic equations* such as 'breast = world'. Remember Klein's case of Little Dick (Klein, 1932),[2] in which Klein interprets according to such equations, e.g. big train = daddy, station = mummy, etc. From that point on, if Klein and Lacan could shake hands about positing an imaginary order (when saying that part of psychic reality is imaginary in so far as it is based on imaginary constructions), their paths separate as to the function of the symbolic order.

With her analytical work with children Klein had set herself the unique task of exploring the most primordial objects of the imagination in its earliest stages. And that is why they are called objects and not people, humans. There is nothing in very early infancy resembling a human world or another person in its wholeness. This prehuman world is also pre-verbal, a fact which Klein caught by isolating it in her observations of children, hence making of it the cornerstone of her clinical and theoretical work.

But the problem consists precisely in the use she made of her discoveries; that is, in the way in which she brings this newly acquired knowledge into the dynamics (the English would say) or into the dialectics (as the romance-Lacanians would say) within which the subject, both child and adult, refers to a truth which is multiple. This is exactly the allure of the imaginary: it shows the image of objects which are not there; in other words it strives to give an image to the little object *a*.

We can begin to see here a radical difference in the function Kleinians and Lacanians give to phantasy, as well as a conceptual similarity. Klein soon realized that the object she refers to and by means of which she interprets, namely, the maternal breast, is an object which is not there, which is lost, or which we are always losing. Unlike Lacan, who considered the phantasy an element which resists signification and is therefore uninterpretable, for Klein it is rather a question of mounting the phantasies in the attempt to tame them by language; that is, by symbolic equations. Language, the symbolic (her manifold interpretations), descends on the phantasy like a *deus ex machina* and changes it.

This *deus ex machina*, thanks to which the affect is invested in new objects and which separates the baby from the body of the mother, is also a *deus causa sui*, because it is the origin of psychic movement. According to Lacan too, human beings grow up (they do not go on clinging to the nest) because they are introduced into 'new circuits', as Lacan calls them in his seminar on the object-relation (1956–7).

But for Klein and Segal, as we have now seen, symbolization comes to pass by means of equations. They mean that a new symbol will never be acquired if not in an equation with an image already there: the image is the psychic reality, the image of the mother's body.[3] The imaginary acquisition of a good object in the internal world of the patient changes its psychic quality. In practical terms, the object which was lost in the real can be found again in our imagination. But Klein, no less than Lacan, realized that it is this separation from an object that characterizes the human condition. Her direction of the treatment, then, aims on the one hand at a separation from the 'real' of the maternal body. But then she reintroduces the unity in another reality, the phantasmatic reality. A lot of needlework is needed to repair this fundamental division between infant-analysand and mother-analyst: one needs to sew back what has been rent by the aggressive and sadistic phantasies of earliest infancy. And a great deal of thread is needed for the seam to hold strongly. But it is not difficult to realize that what stitches together the imaginary material in Kleinian practice is the thread of discourse; it is the discourse about an object which was lost and then found again in an imaginary aesthetic pathos rather than in a symbolic ethos. We will see how the most eminent Kleinian theoreticians, such as Bion and his pupil Meltzer, are interested in an aesthetic experience of the subject, containing the tragic pathos of beauty.

Coming back to the more classical Kleinians: their work could be defined in terms of giving reality to phantasies through the symbolic power of words. But it is only when one is aware of this special power of words, power which all analysts use but without knowing that they are using it, that one is a Lacanian (and would therefore make a minimal use of it).

The case of O.R.

It was a clash in its most passionate form, and it was evident from the beginning. O.R. was demanding an analysis with which she would disagree. She was in radical disagreement with her father, whom she described as cutting and malevolent, the way at times O.R. presented herself to me. Her rage seemed often only a way to distract me from her fits of genuine surprise at my interventions. In contrast with her unweighed reactions, she devoted a detailed attention to my interventions by describing to me the difference between them and what she was expecting. In the end, it was with this attentive and passionate analysand that I learned how my work was different from that of my English colleagues.

O.R.'s demands in this first stage of analysis fitted with the Kleinian understanding of the impassioned state as she had experienced it in a previous psychotherapy. But whereas the latter responded to her demand of a loving fusion with the mother, in this analysis she demanded me in the function of *container* for all her hate of the absolute other. The other she hated was mainly the man, who imposed his hard, obsessional and at the same time arbitrary law. But there was also a question of the Other/mother, this supposed container which is fused and confused with the subject in an interchangeable and identificatory relation.

The passage to the couch

Once she admitted that she could not stop her recriminations against me, in spite of her good will. She was announcing her imminent fit of rage before hurling it against me; but it was precisely by telling me that she suspended the compulsive act. We both found ourselves as interlocutors in a logical time (Lacan, 1966c):[4] its suspension for her (the time to speak suspended the time to act in), and a time to reach a conclusion for me. Her time to understand was offering me a time to act. I showed her the couch with a 'What if . . . ?' and she looked at me as if I had gone out of my mind, how could I even think . . . ? I just patted the cushion of the couch. Was I joking? Could I even dream of using such an authoritarian gesture with her? But there she was at the same time, lying down in a state of wonder and bliss in front of the empty wall. And it was through the intermediary of this empty wall that a new phase started in her analysis.

It was not long after the passage to the couch that another not less important and stormy session took place. We were commenting on some of her dreams which she had reported the time before, and about which she had written a short poem. This seemed to her very meaningful, but she was not able to interpret it, and it provoked in her very strong emotions. Suddenly she turned and pointed her gaze towards me, asking me if I wanted to see it. And to her surprise no less than mine the refusal appeared. What was this refusal about? I have nothing against poetry and at other times in similar situations I have taken it in good part. How was it that this time I refused to offer my gaze? Maybe because I wanted to frustrate the analysand's demand to have me interpreting in this way, or maybe out of counter-transferential spite? Certainly these were the elements she was calling into play, by means of which she was provoking my passion or counter-transference, by means of which she was putting me to the test, as it were. By re-establishing the dimension of the gaze, her own pointed at me, and mine to be offered, the passage to the couch was to be put in question; that is, the passage from a time to look to a time to understand. What was in question was the dropping of the gaze, the object of fusion. This time, taken by surprise, I had to conclude with a suspension, with an analytical act of refusal. I acted as if pathos itself had to reveal itself bluntly and barely to blind me. The subject, by demanding the gaze (an object, for a Lacanian) which was appealing to my aesthetic pathos, was seducing me with the object-art, with its 'very strong emotions', with her *jouissance*.

So I discovered this brutality of mine which responded to the imperative demand of the other's *jouissance*. The impossibility of responding to the appeal of passion, whether explicit or masked, seemed to have created a breaking and surprising act. This can also account sometimes for the theoretical and clinical stiffening and lack of spontaneity in the 'professional' attitude of some analysts. Here the *savoir faire* of the analyst is called into play, for the analytical response emerges precisely from this impossibility of meeting the demand which the analytical dialectic itself provokes. We must not confuse, then, this lack of response to a demand with a theoretical dogma but, on the contrary, discover it as a surprising necessity. To do it as a matter of course is to lose some of the effectiveness of a non-response, the surprise indeed.[5]

She felt alive only when she was in some sort of opposition to me; only then did she feel she existed in opposition to the obsessional organization of her work and her life. She was asking for her *self* according to her dialectic of opposition to the other. In the previous therapy she had agreed to a fusion with mother thanks to a process of interpretations which we could call 'maternal', centred on the mother–daughter relationship. But what she really feared was what she called 'the leap' in her very first session, this leap from this game for two, which object-relations therapy is, into a larger game with at least two other players: father and death.

A few sessions later she said, 'My parents never gave any order to me overtly but, if I had not done what they wanted, it would have been either my or their death, the end of any relation to them. They had me but nobody knew it.' Hence we could say that in this case transference functioned in this way: in the first instance, she had, by clashing with me, refused the maternal transference: I was *the one who did not know* her relation to her mother (as well as her previous therapist did). But with the couch move I passed into the position of the one who knows by preserving the parents' real authority in a 'central void', in front of a wall.

In the last session claustrophobic fears appeared and a dream where she was exploring exotic spaces with strange animals. For the first time she talked about her brother; she suddenly realized that the small circuit was occupied by at least another person and that she was not uniquely necessary to mother. She suddenly realized that like a ball she was thrown into the paternal obsessionality to whose insignia she clung and identified hysterically: academic work and intellect, which she passionately refused. She was looking for a self which did not stem from the other's necessity, and it was this hostility to the other which represented a certain authenticity for her, even though in the negative. But what she found at a certain point of her analysis was the emptiness both of the wall and of the place of the analyst.

It is on the empty screen that will appear all the faces, masks, characters and objects with which that place has been filled by the analysand. J. McDougall (1986) called it 'Theatres of the mind on the psychoanalytical stage'. The *metteur en scène*, the director, is the analysand, but the stage manager is the analyst, with her/his draconian rules about keeping her/himself and her/his own masks and characters offstage. It is not the attempt to unmask and hunt down anything which does the trick. On the contrary, it is done by letting the masks, the legends, fictions and phantasies appear from the place which was supposed to be filled up by an unapproachable authority (as it was by O.R.'s parents, then by myself). Masks and characters, then, appear and fall, only to leave another mask in their place; as in Pirandello's poetics, where under a mask there is another mask, the analyst should know that there is nothing to unmask but the masks themselves, *for being only masks*.

Once all the allurements which had been filling that place have exhausted their function of cork, that place will appear as a hole. At this appearance of the hole, in the Other, in the silence which follows, we witness the most intimate contact of the subject with itself. It is from this silence that desire emerges beside passion. If words have helped this emptying, the silence pertains to the encounter with the Other in its purity as nothing else than the other part of us which we have disavowed, the forbidden Medusa who can petrify with her gaze. Death is finally encountered in the form of the unspeakable. In this encounter with death one's own being is put dejectedly in question. All we shall find in this place is the person of the analyst, occupying the place of the object (a), the bodily relic left over from a once alluring phantasmic bubble.

This is the second stage in a transference whose problematic is love and not passion, as we will see. An analyst like Winnicott, for example, believes in a self, just as O.R. was looking for an essence of her self, an ultimate authenticity lost in the many layers of the world's falseness. According to Winnicott, the outside and ourselves deceive us about ourselves. But how is it possible that such thinkers of the best English empiricist school can choose as their object of work, of science and knowledge, the self, such an impalpable, unreachable and untouchable identity; how to demonstrate its existence, that a true self exists beyond these crusts which make a real crustacean out of the subject, a self with a tangible form?

According to Winnicott, if we cannot touch the essence of the subject with our own hands, like the apostle St Thomas, we can at least feel it; the feeling is the tangible and concrete evidence of the soul, as it were. But what St Thomas had to touch in order to be convinced that Christ was there, whole and alive, were his wounds, the openings on his body. He could believe that Christ was really there, not as God – intact in his appearance – but only as a man, with the evidence of suffering: his blood and passion. Poor Thomas, so engrossed in the passion of Christ, missed the fact that Christ was risen. Engrossed in his own gaze, his specular reflection of humanity, he wanted to see himself in the wounds of God, and in so doing he was missing God, his message of salvation, of rising from passion.

Thomas is the patient, the one who is subjected to pathos, who suffers from passion. He is the one who, in front of the message of salvation (of cure), of the possibility of ceasing to bleed, of turning one's own envious gaze from the miseries of the other, does not cease to bleed, remains transfixed, morbidly horrified, pathologized in front of his own symptom reflected in the body of the other.

Why? We could also ask why the patient is fixed in his childhood's problematics in the way psychoanalysis, whether Kleinian or Lacanian, does not cease to demonstrate. Why is there resistance to going over the traumatic experience, however painful, even when it has ceased to be present? Why did St Thomas not rejoice at the sight of the risen God, why did he doubt the fact of his presence?

What is this passion for the symptom, this repetition of the suffering, of the past, of childhood?

Analysts of the object-relations school deal with it as a nostalgia which ties the subject to the lost object in an impossible repetition. The problem with this conceptual approach is that there is no way out: it is an object which they believe was there once, the mother's breast, and it determined the relation of the baby to the world. The breast is the world *in nuce*, its kernel, and a real unsatisfactory relation to the breast makes the world bad for Winnicott. For Winnicott there is no death drive. The breast can only be accidentally unsatisfactory because it is conceived of as the good in itself, as all the child needs and demands. Thus Winnicott believes it is only by a counter-experience, and analysis is one such possibility, that the baby is given the chance of relating to the object-world in a better way.

The world encloses itself around the circular surface of the breast; even in analysis the analysts identify themselves with a breast, possibly a good one, and, at times, also with a nipple, a bottle or a containing potty. The literal unfolding of these metaphors seems to be a necessary condition for the cure. Maybe that is why not even Jesus could avoid Thomas's pathos, because he did not show him the breasts that even Christ does not have. But Thomas was an apostle, a saint, after all; Christ must have taught him something, even breastless. Or maybe because of it, by showing his holes in the body, he was pointing at something else, or at the fact that *something was not there*. In the place of the fullness of the breast Thomas found, in anguish, gaps of flesh. That was Christ's therapy.

The object and the other

Let us come back to Lacan, to the scheme he gave us in his seminar 'La relation d'objet' (1956–7). In this, he indicates the three stages relating to a possible process of relation to the object. I am trying to go back to the imaginary, both Kleinian and Lacanian, in order to show that it gives a foundation to passion as a correlate of the demand for love. We have, then, these stages:

1 Identification with the object of the maternal desire (desire of the desire of the mother). The child is here in the position of a

mirage, as the object of the mother's desire. Here one is subjected more than subject, subjected to the other's movements.
Here we posit passion (for the object which is not one's own)
and Winnicott's 'false self', which speaks from the place of the
other.

2 The full Oedipus: the father intervenes, depriving the child of
the mother; it is the encounter with the law. Here we posit the
Shakespearian problematic of being or not being (the phallus),
as the object of maternal desire is put in question by the father's
interdiction.

3 The decline of Oedipus, when the father possesses and is not the
Phallus, and gives it symbolically to the child; he is the giver of
a law whose object is not real but symbolic. Beyond the dual relation a third term is introduced, through which the subject can
demand to be recognized, signified. This is symbolic castration.
By subjecting ourselves to it we lose something, but gain our
right to be recognized as subjects. Castration becomes a sign of
recognition like a tattoo or a circumcision, and it is not a primordial aggressive drive, but the preservation of desire for what is
lost.

If the third stage is an attempt at resolving the second one, it is the
first that remains problematic, certainly for Klein and Winnicott but
also for the Lacanians. If Lacanian analysts point at the last two this
does not mean that they can do without the first. Lacanian analyses
also last for years, get stuck like any other, exactly because it is this
first stage that interferes, returns, insists and makes both analysand
and analyst despair, just like a passion, a real suffering. Can we try
to describe this stage, as Lacan did try after all, without falling into
the trap of the Kleinian containment and quest for this primordial object/breast, or of the quest of so many other researchers in
this field for the uterine cloister and pre-birth states, and why not,
I should add, as far as the scattered molecules of matter before
conception?

In the end we know that this object is lost in the meanderings of
time, of all times; it is the mythical object, always already lost, and
all these other objects into which we try to fix the original one are
nothing else but substitutes, representatives at various levels of the
object which does not exist. But they are taken for this lost object,
whose memory, according to Winnicott, keeps us sane. This is the

background to his concept of the transitional object. But for the Lacanians it is the opposite. It is this stubborn memory, this fixation, that drives us mad; it is this being drawn back in that stops us progressing, this passion for the past, this passion of childhood.[6]

But if this passion is, for the British school, a matter of fact, which only a psychic education can alter, it is not less so for Lacan, who on the other hand tries to understand why and in what this psychic education consists. Lacan explains the fundamental dependence on the Other through the prematuration of birth,[7] which not only marks us as inadequate beings, but also marks our relationship to the Other as a dependent one. The Other makes us exist, but only at the cost of making our survival depend on itself. Thus the problem is turned upside down: it is not a question of a primordial object, but of a vital dependence of our existence on the *existence* of the Other.

At a primordial stage, one cannot speak of an object as one cannot even speak of a subject: this is the transitivistic phase of non-distinction from the other. An image of one's own distinction from the other is constituted at the Mirror Stage, which from insufficiency pushes us to anticipation of our subjectivity in the form of an ego, imaginary subject. The other becomes, therefore, the specular double, the little other, as little as me.

But the doubling is triple as the other still retains his/her essence of big Other; that is, the one without whom we do not subsist. Yet, at the same time, it is also the other *like me* dependent on the support of another like me and, therefore, redundant, excessive. It is difficult to come out of this excess. The other remains the one who does not lack, and for whom I am only an object, his/her slave, and at the same time, like me, s/he needs me because s/he lacks, and what is worse, it is not me s/he lacks (in case my function of support should fail); in the end s/he lacks in spite of me. This doubling of the other is not to be undervalued, for any relation to the other, not only to the analyst, hides this duplicity. The absolute Other is challenged, implored and idealized; it is idealized but only in order to create a radical resentment towards another like me for having such a stature in relation to me. The big Other is always potentially a little other, it is always to be dethroned in neurosis.

The more the other tries to mask this reciprocal lacking, the more the anguish emerges and the more, too, does the awareness of an inadequacy without a way out. In the end, the more this other contains the more it becomes one's own prison; often, a *folie à deux*. In other words it is the addiction to the object of the other, that which confirms one's own lack of independence and the consequent desire to make it disappear in order to affirm, thus, one's own completeness and unity, this famous self. We want, then, to be more than half, primarily because there is no other half which holds, the other being irreducibly Other at this point of the process. Lacan has pointed out how to emerge from this impasse, this chaos with the other, and to re-establish or encounter an order. This passion for the other is to be placed, for Lacan, in the passage from alienation to separation from the other (mother); the symbolic order is encountered in the father, who transcends the dual relation without exit and marks a subjection in which a name, a place and a law are given to the child.

But let us ask ourselves what happens to the mother in this second stage. And let us be aware also of the fact that this is a problem that the Kleinian theoreticians pose also. According to them too, what reconciles the subject to the world is a gift: the good internal object for them (the phallus for the Lacanians). But what happens to this mother who was so passionately loved? No analyst denies that a profound nostalgia for something which was lost remains. In a Lacanian perspective the absent mother, the one who frustrates, who does not respond to her child's demands (or only when she feels like it) becomes *real*; she decays from being the imaginary big Other and becomes real power; she is the sphinx, the two-headed monster, the cannibal witch, Medusa. What has happened to that wonderful lost object?

For Meltzer (1984) this object was never so much a good object as a beautiful one. It is the tragic beauty of the breast and of the lost maternal body that we seek in art and in aesthetic experience generally. It seems to be close to what Hegel called tragic pathos: a dialectical return to the original passion through the human law, thanks to which passion becomes aesthetic pathos. It is in fact through consciousness that, for Hegel, the primary passion, the underworld, realizes itself on earth as positive and not destructive existence (Hegel, 1967). In the Hegelian dialectic, nothing is destroyed, even the primary *real* passion is rational and coexists as a dialectic opposition, which is the *conditio sine qua non* for the 'in-itself' and 'for-itself' to exist. Lacan revisited Hegel in his dialectic of the object-relation only where pathos is met by the tragic ethos.[8]

If passion, via the human law, has become pathos, that is, love for an unreachable 'real', this is possible only thanks to an ethical passion. This ethical passion makes of the absent mother not a monster but a giver; the object, from being the object of satisfaction, becomes a gift; the objects, from being *real*, become symbolic gifts of love. It is at this point that the symbol is introduced together with the ethical quality of the subject. This is the power of absence where the object, the signified, does not signify anything if it is not marked by a signifier; this is the ethical power of absence which turns love from something we are always demanding into a gift that is received. This is also where the ethics of desire resides, this desire which is never evident in analysis, unlike passion, for it is immediately alienated in the demand. Desire is discovered in analysis as a residue between need and the demand to be loved by the other. Desire springs from a passion, what Lacan called the 'passion of the signifier', through which we can subject ourselves to a law which transcends passions. Transcended passion is pathos, which is passion's dramatization, Greek tragedy; it is the material of desire. The relationship to the other is mediated by desire as it is the residue of a separation, the space which was left empty between the subject and the other (like the space filled by O.R.'s gaze). This empty space makes it possible to come out of the specular and pre-specular alienation from the other. It does so because it abolishes the supremacy of this other, who then becomes irreducible in its otherness, rather than always complementary. This, of course, does not mean getting rid of the other, but passing from a subject–object relation to one between subject and subject.

To return to the problem with which we began: if our demanding is there from the beginning, and if demand is always the demand for love, then love is implicated in the passionate state. We could roughly call it *love-passion*, in opposition to *love-desire*. Love-passion is the hate underlying any good resolution, any idealization of the other who keeps us dependent; this is the love of the slave, in an imaginary relation to a master who is always resented. Love-desire is knowing that we love that which not only have we not got, but which the other does not have either. It is to give what we do not have, if we do not want to deceive our beloved.

In the place of the passion for an impossible unity with the object, love bonds two people who cannot be united together, between whom the possibility of hate, of a fracture and division, is always possible.

Now we can perhaps ask if the end of analysis coincides with the end of hate. Maybe Winnicott (1989) gives us a good example in his case of the 'Piggle' (see chapter 8). At the termination of the little girl's analysis, in one of his characteristic ludic interpretations Winnicott pushes the girl away from him and exclaims 'I hate you.' Then the little Piggle gets hold of two curtains and runs into the middle of the room and shouts, 'I am the wind, look!' Is it this hate from which Winnicott separates her by articulating it that frees the Piggle also from her own analysis? Maybe this is love for Winnicott: the effect of a separation which implies hate, a liberation from passion dependence, which Lacan defined as 'this knot of imaginary servitude which love has always to undo again and sever', a knot that 'psychoanalysis alone recognizes' because 'the sufferings of neurosis and psychosis are for us a schooling in the passions of the soul' (1977d, p. 7).

Interlude: Madness in Philosophy, or Derrida's Love of Lacan

But we are travelling too far with love. It is time to go back to knowledge and to mystery. The philosopher thinks about the mystery of the world. According to Descartes the only certainty that human knowledge possesses about this mystery is the certainty that humans can *think about* the world. But what about the world itself? Can thought know it? We do not have the guarantee that the external world, as we know (perceive) it, *is*, that is, possesses 'being'. But the one who thinks the world does: the thinker *is*. In Lacanian terms we could call the Cartesian 'being' a *'pens-être'*, a 'thinking being'.[1]

Descartes establishes the certainty of 'being' in the subject who thinks. Whether what is thought 'is' or 'is not', that is, whether thought and its contents coincide, is a problem of God's good will. Descartes broke with the Aristotelian dichotomy which involves, for example, that of matter and form. Aristotle resolved his own dualism with the concept of the *'sunolon'*: two elements which constitute a whole, a One. The Aristotelian *sunolon* was opposed to the Platonic doctrine, where reality is to be attributed only to forms or universals whose existence is considered independent of the objects, which represent them only imperfectly. For Aristotle, matter is the determined potentiality of objects. They become actual only thanks to the activity of forms, and the form exists only in its objects. Lacan does not believe in this unitary and harmonious Aristotelian world. The Platonic form lends itself better to Lacanian algorithms. There, it can retain the determinant position of a signifier above the bar. Thus:

$$\frac{\text{forms}}{\text{objects}}$$

This means that what is above the bar (the forms) determines what is under (the objects, the signified).

The problem of dichotomies is a symptomatic effect of an irreducible division in the world (between its reality and its representations, or between thought and perception, reason and experience, being and non-being): centuries of philosophical debate have attempted to find a solution, a point of repair. And whether that be a hidden unity of the terms in question or the predominance of one over the other, philosophy offers ways of dealing with the dichotomous fracture between 'being' and truth. This 'deal' is the philosophical practice, the thinker's ethics, which is not without its effects. It is not without 'therapeutic' effects since, like psychoanalysis, it relies on effects of truth. We shall come back to this therapeutic aspect of the philosophical practice, this *cura sui* whose effect is supposed to be wisdom (Foucault, 1976–84).

So the dualistic fracture is the source of the philosophical quest, a quest for primacy, a primary signifier that will give meaning to this fracture.

The dualistic polemic goes back as far as the early naturalistic pre-Socratic philosophies, which described their principles on the basis of a priority of matter, the natural elements. It was up to Plato to introduce the primacy of forms, and for Aristotle to introduce the harmonious Whole. The conflict between these two visions of the world was settled elegantly by Hegel centuries later with his formula, 'All that is real is rational, and all that is rational is real.' This formula does not stray very far from the Aristotelian *sunolon*. According to both Aristotle and Hegel, there was a concordance of progression between real and rational, form and matter, the world and the intellect who thinks it. Empiricism also allies itself to this philosophy of the 'consensus', common sense, consent, agreement between these two phenomena of the world. In empirical terms our experience agrees with the reality we experience, whereas the most rigorous opponent of this philosophical conception was Descartes's rationalism. Reason is for Descartes real, and only reason is real. There is no Hegelian equivalence of 'being' between real and rational. Not only is reality not rational at all but, on the contrary, reality, as perceived by our senses, is what deceives us, what drives us out of reason: we could say – mad. It was precisely to the Cartesian possibility of madness as the limit of reason that Foucault paid attention. Madness represents for Descartes the uttermost model of deception; it is the extreme position of slavery to the illusions of the senses.

We must look more carefully into this opposition between reason and madness, as Foucault has suggested, and as Derrida has done in his essay 'Cogito and history of madness' (1990): a polemical reply to Foucault's suggestion in his book *Madness and Civilisation* (1971). Let us imagine a conversation about madness between Descartes, Foucault and Derrida.[2] Foucault supports the idea that, in the 'Meditations', Descartes (1984) excluded the possibility of madness (mental derangement) from methodological doubt. We can summarize Descartes's exclusion of madness in one sentence: 'You can doubt everything, but only on condition that you are not mad.' Foucault brings forth this Cartesian consideration as the philosophical expression of 'Le grand renfermement', the great confinement of madness in the classical age, whereas for Derrida, Descartes is the inaugurator of the split between the two modern currents of empiricism and rationalism, experience and reason, reality and representations.

Consider Descartes's methodical doubt: he wonders whether our sense-images through which we perceive reality might all be like the illusory images of a dream. Unlike empiricists he does not trust experience. All experiences could be errors and illusions of the senses. What can be trusted, then, if all our experiences may deceive us? How find certainty? If truth does not reside in the senses, where is truth? Where is that last element which does not let itself be dissolved into illusions? We shall only know it if we doubt, 'methodically', everything. By doubting, Descartes sets off in search of certainty. He looks for it outside the territory of the senses, barring them from any possibility of knowledge.[3] But we can find even in the most bizarre and unreal dream something which cannot be reduced to imagination, something irreducible to error, such as, for example, the existence of colour, which is a primary element, which cannot be decomposed. So there must be units which are not experienced but are understood by the intellect. The prototypes of this understanding are mathematics and those sciences which deal with very general and simple things, without concern about whether they exist or not in nature.

It follows for Descartes that only the principles which regulate experience are true. But in order to find these principles, these last elements which cannot be doubted, Descartes had to proceed by exclusion, by doubting everything as an effect of our illusions. It is a search for certainty, based on a lack of concern for reality as perceived by our senses. It is a certainty born of doubt: I can doubt everything, but I cannot doubt that I doubt. By doubting I come across the certainty of my doubting. And what is this passage from doubt to certainty but the effect of my thought? Only thought turns doubt into certainty; even the certainty of my own existence comes only from thought. I can doubt my existence, as it may be only an illusion of my common sense, but I cannot doubt that I doubt my existence. This operation of thought becomes the only guarantor of truth. Truth is the certainty of 'being': for Cartesian philosophy truth is ontological. Certainty of truth is certainty of being, of the fact that 'I am.'

In the 'I think therefore I am' thought, truth and being coincide. What matters is not to demonstrate that there is a thinker, or this particular being called Descartes, because the existence of the person who is thinking is proved only by the fact that s/he thinks. I know that I am only because I think.

But to 'I can doubt everything', Descartes adds, 'provided I am not mad, and provided that I am not dreaming.' Mad people and dreamers are the opposite of the doubter, or the thinker. They have no authority over thought because they are *certain* of their illusions. Psychotics do not doubt their delusions or dreamers their onirocal images while they are asleep; therefore their certainties do not count in an assessment of human knowledge. Foucault interprets this position as the major rejection of madness effected by philosophy. But Derrida comes in to rescue Descartes from this interpretation. According to Derrida, Descartes used the example of madness only to rescue himself from being considered mad because of his ideas. The 'Meditations' are exactly the form of monologue which hides the dialogue Descartes is engaged in with a potential interlocutor. It is a bit like the case of Socrates' interlocutors in Plato's dialogues: the other interlocutor is there only as the fool on duty. He represents the non-philosopher, or the common-sense philosopher who tries to challenge the daring thinker with questions such as 'Are you mad in doubting that all we perceive is illusory?' 'No', Descartes answers, 'as I am here writing and being listened to, I am not mad and neither are you. So we are sane people. Madness is not what reveals the fragility of my ideas.'

Derrida points out another facet of Descartes's use of the word madness; a more conversational, familiar use of it, such as 'You must be mad if you think in such a bizarre way.' So Descartes's answer also implied that those normal men who believe blindly in the appearances of things, in the way their senses perceive them, and who cannot doubt their limited and deceiving good sense are the real fools, not him! Madness would be here only a rhetorical being in the wrong, a form of rudeness towards the opponent. But here again we come across the conception that madness corresponds to being in the wrong. Derrida's rescue does not save Descartes from Foucault's criticism but instead adds more fuel to his fire: madness cannot be taken into consideration in Cartesian thought unless it is on the wrong side, whether that be the psychotic in the madhouse or the neurotic common-sense thinker in the office. So madness appears in Descartes's system as that which cannot contribute to the knowledge of the world. It is rational waste, like the absurdity of dreams in the economy of our mental life. Madness belongs to those who do not doubt, who are outside the possibility of being deceived, to those who cannot constitute themselves subjects of knowledge.

Which side does psychoanalysis take? Where is truth for psychoanalysis – on the side of madness or on the side of thought? On the side of the dreamer or of the one awake? Psychoanalysis does not take either of these two sides, and that is why it is not a philosophy. Philosophy is always a vision of the world. It can affirm itself only by means of the exclusion of other visions. Philosophy is grounded in thought, and any truth it might be hunting will always be a truth belonging to a particular thought. Psychoanalysis starts at the point where philosophy finds its limits. It goes beyond thought as it discovers the action of the unthought, of the unconscious indeed. Psychoanalysis is not thought but act, a practice. That does not mean that thought is not involved in this practice. On the contrary, by listening to what his patients had to say Freud realized that there was something beyond thought, which not only interferes with it but is so intermingled with thought that it is difficult to tell one from the other. 'I am where I don't think', says Lacan, reversing the Cartesian terms. Being and thought do not coincide. Thought carries on thinking in vain. This is Lacan's challenge to philosophy.

And philosophy goes on thinking . . . that it cannot think 'being' any more; it carries on thinking about the discoveries of the practice which psychoanalysis is. Psychoanalysis has not taken sides between thought and madness. It listens to both. It does not reject madness or what interferes with rational or logical thought. It does not exclude madness in thought.

Is it not exactly the possibility of madness which Descartes fears, when he wants to demonstrate his mental sanity, so that his ideas can be better accepted? 'As I am here doing normal things, writing and communicating, I am not mad.' But people who are clinically mad can still do normal things and, so far as writing and communicating are concerned, they do it a lot. But we do not take them into account, just as Descartes did not. Is it not part of a popular myth that the artist, the genius, the great scientist are, if not clinically mad, at least eccentric? They are supposed to be, and justified by being different, uncommon indeed. But in cases like Nietzsche, Hölderlin, Artaud, we can see that their clinical madness did not prevent them from being among the finest voices of our contemporary age, carriers of a madness which has produced thought and, at the same time, troubled the individuals in question. Psychoanalysis, like a rationalist, does not assume a harmony of the world or an agreement between its different aspects. But it is empiricist in its method of detecting and listening to the uncommon, to that which is discordant and unthought. It does not reject this disagreement but takes it on.

Psychoanalysis does not believe that one and one makes a big One. It is not Aristotelian. On the contrary, it places itself in the crack of a division. From this divided position, reality and thought do not seem to have the same preponderance. The psychoanalytic experience has touched upon other places which the upholders of either reason or reality had excluded from their field of vision. Psychoanalysis may be called, perhaps, 'real-ism', as it has discovered that beside and between reality and its representations there is the 'real', what is impossible in reality, but nevertheless possible outside of it. There is an out-of-it, out of the dichotomy. There is the other place which one can never enter unless one solves the insoluble riddle that Zen teachers call the *Koan*, the riddle that is the mystery of initiation into the 'real', that state which escapes any attempt at being represented, thought, symbolized. This out-of-it state, this ex-stasis, participates in the nature of the ineffable, belongs to the excluded area of non-being. Maybe psychoanalysis has learned from the madness of its patients to doubt 'being'. Psychoanalysis cannot enter into the history of philosophy as an ontology, as a thought concerned with the truth of being, but only as that which challenges this conviction. The fact that 'I think that I am' does not mean that 'I really am.' I can still only know my capacity to think, but I will not know anything about my 'being', which appears to owe its right 'to be' only to thought. Lacan made a nice pun on the word 'being' to show that the ontology is the discourse of *m'être*/ *maître*, of the ego-being/master. The master in the guise of the ego says that one must 'be' in order to be taken seriously. Being is the master's requirement. The master demands (pretends) knowledge about 'being' without realizing that it cannot be thought in the language of sane human beings. That is perhaps why Descartes feared being taken for a madman. Lacan has instead opposed to being 'the Thing', which appears only when all has been said, only when thoughts have found themselves at their wits' end. The solution of the riddle is the end of representation; it is the last word before acceding to the Thing.

The master is the one who imposes the truth of being on its scientific, ideological, technical knowledge. Psychoanalysis unmasks the concept of 'being' as belonging to the field of reality in which only that which is real is true. Otherwise you are mad, like those who believe that their hallucinations are true. Psychoanalysis unmasks the 'either . . . or' of the master, when one is faced with the choice 'either your freedom or your life' for example. One can choose one's freedom and one loses one's life. Or one can choose one's life, but one has still lost it because it does not belong to oneself any more, but to someone who by now has become one's master. But, however absurd the choice given, one is left with no choice but to reply to it. Madness is one way of replying to a choice. So is suicide. The possibilities of choosing not to be, in a world whose conditions one has not accepted, or of releasing oneself from one's own duty to choose (that is, to exist), are always present. As we saw in the last chapters, the psychoanalytic discourse is not ontological but ethical. Its concern is not with the truth of 'being' but with the truth of our choices. It deals with a truth which cannot be expressed philosophically, because it is not of the same order of thought as *cogito*, as presence to itself. Psychoanalysis, rather, is a truth 'in action' or 'of action' as it engages the utterance of our demands and replies. Speech is the act of answering for one's own actions, for one's own choices.

So in its practice psychoanalysis brings its own subject into being: not one who thinks (and is supposed to be knowing) but one who acts by way of speech. Psychoanalysis, with its modest, partial truth which appears and disappears, so unstable, unfaithful and capricious, but none the less active and therapeutic in any of its flashing bits, is the real breakthrough of philosophy. Psychoanalysis might be the last form of that *cura sui*, cure (or care) of the soul, which the wise westerner sought in philosophy. And every philosophy, being love of knowledge, is an ethics which is the therapy of the lost soul. Marx wanted philosophy to change the world rather than just to interpret it. With Freud we have the philosophical reversal of the century: there are interpretations which change the soul. Psychoanalysis is an interpretation of thought which changes philosophy. As Derrida puts it himself in his 'Pour l'amour de Lacan', 'Lacan has put on the scene the singular desire of the philosopher. In this way he has helped open the space of a new philosophical culture. In which we are, even though they want to make us forget it in order to go back to the other side' (1991, p. 403: my translation).

Part II

4

Hysteria: Comedy . . . dell'Arte

When we go into analysis we go to meet a perfect stranger. It is to her/him that we address our demands, questions and implorings. But we address the other only to meet our own questions, demands and implorings. It is precisely this questioning, which hunts yet fails to catch the answer, that is always at the core of the psychoanalytical experience. And this core is never encountered in its essence but is, rather, always veiled. At times the analyst finds her/himself confronted with armour, at other times with golden brocade, and, perplexed, gazes at it, but there it is, always, a tear hidden within the folds of the drape. Only a whisper at times unmasks its presence. And once you have this tear in your hands, all that appears to you is not the beauty behind the veil, but a cry, an unutterable question, a symptom.

The holed sheet

This reminds me of one of Salman Rushdie's characters in his novel *Midnight's Children*, Saleem Sinai's grandfather, when, as a young doctor, his grandfather was asked to examine a sick girl. As he was shown by the girl's father into a big dark room, all he could see was a big sheet held by two women looking like wrestlers. What was he supposed to do in the presence of this sheet? Very simple, the father explained: this was a perforated sheet and his sick daughter was behind it, as was to be expected of a good girl. All the doctor had to do was to 'specify which portion of [her] it [was] necessary to inspect', and the father would 'then issue her with [his] instructions to place the required segment against that hole' in the sheet, 'and so, in this fashion the thing [might] be achieved' (1982, p. 23), the father concluded. What there was in fact to achieve was his daughter's marriage with the promising young doctor. Many more illnesses followed the first one: for every new illness a further examination by the doctor, for every new part of the body against the hole another step towards marriage. The good hysterical girl will become Saleem's grandmother.

Here we have all the elements for a novel as well as for a paper about feminine sexuality, hysteria and comedy. In this story we have the role of physician and lover merging together. As for the role of the physician, in this case we can see the similarity to the analyst's: all the doctor could see of his patient were diseased pieces of her body against the hole in a sheet which hid her, whereas as a lover, all he could see of the girl's femininity was the sheet which covered it.

Saleem's grandmother was not ugly, but not a particularly desirable woman, especially once she became grandfather's wife. She was never as beautiful and desirable as when she played her comedy hiding behind the sheet. And if you think that the lover was aroused by the pieces of body he was allowed to examine, you would not be completely wrong, because the function of her illness was to tantalize the lover by covering with a symptom the only hole through which he hoped to look at the whole of her healthy beauty. This resembles the hysterical symptom: there where the body is involved with desire, both the other's or one's own, it stops functioning, it becomes ill, and therefore undesirable.

What about the rest of the body? We do not know, as it is always hidden away; it is this very hiding; it is rather like hide-and-seek: blindfold you chase somebody of whom you triumphantly get hold, just to let him/her go. In the game it is not this person you are interested in, but his/her function of prey, and your triumph.

The good girl behind the sheet knew this very well; it belonged to the social game of marriage and conquest. Unlike with hide-and-seek, she had to be chased in order to triumph. Her femininity functioned in absentia, to become a cold and bitter housewife once she was uncovered. Is it a joke, this symptom which, like a jack-in-the-box, mocks you out of your disappointment?

The problem is that a symptom is not a joke, even when it has all the artful embroidery of some hysterical symptoms. What puzzled

Freud, when dealing with hysterical patients, was the fact that hysteria, this assumed typically feminine disturbance, never showed any femininity if not as an unrevealable secret, and, as he could not find any unconscious representation of feminine libido in his patients, he had to conclude that sexual libido is only masculine. Like Rushdie's character, all Freud could come to terms with were his patients' diseased pieces of body, as if they were displayed through the hole of their conversion symptoms. It is only by hiding behind their crumbs of flesh that hysterical women reveal themselves as non-existent, as Lacan would have it. And do not believe that Freud was more professional or less taken in by his patients than the Indian doctor was. Freud must have wished to see this femininity, as he went through all the motions of the disappointed lover; he nicely evoked this femininity for them, as when he wanted to teach Dora that girls are made for boys and that, consequently, she was made for Mr K. And all he got from Dora – if not the slap Mr K. received at the lake – was certainly the sack, he was dismissed.

The hysteric, unlike Rushdie's cunning Indian girl who deceives blatantly, is in conflict with her own deception. Dora complied with Freud's arguments while pushing them to their extreme consequences, to the point of mockery. If, from Freud's arguments, one could deduce that patients too are made for doctors and servants for their masters, Dora showed that it does not contradict another point of view, that is, that Freud and Mr K. were not made for her, and so it might well be the case that boys are not made for girls, or doctors for patients, and ultimately, no nosy psychoanalyst is made for femininity. Freud learned the lesson and had to admit defeat: the mystery of the nature of femininity constitutes a theoretical problem, and it was Lacan's task to tackle it from there.[1]

So, paradoxically, if the symptoms of Rushdie's character aimed at covering the mystery of femininity as the support of social conventions which make of it a value of exchange, Dora's symptoms aimed at uncovering this mystification without her knowing it. Behind Dora's symptoms peeps out the possibility of femininity, but it peeps as a failure. The hysterical symptom disrupts the game while playing it. As Freud rightly pointed out to her, she had been a perfect accomplice of father's game of exchange between Mr K. and himself and all her anger against father was basically a displacement of her anger against herself. The hysteric is torn between playing the game and abhorring it; she is torn between a compliance with the symbolic dimension of father and disagreement with it. She identifies with the human order of father only to find that it is according to this order that she, as a woman, functions as a social object of exchange.

Dora is a purist and really believes that femininity is something, that Woman exists, and not, as the Indian girl believed, that femininity is only crumbs of flesh. Dora wanted to be loved all and whole: not this or that, not objects or parts but rather their whole images. She loved photographs and presents. Dora's 'Noli me tangere' disquieted Freud as the young Indian doctor was disquieted. Both girls put themselves behind a veil, both denied their bodies to the man, but for different reasons: one in order to be married, the other in order to be a virgin. They both bypass sex in order to remain whole. They deny the split that human sexuality implies. Whereas Mrs Sinai will be filled by motherhood, Dora loves the Virgin Mother. Virginity is the apology of femininity. This self-enclosed wholeness, and Mary's pregnancy without sex, are the mystery of femininity beyond flesh, and beyond male desire too. Was Dora to desire the presence of Mr K. and wish to speak to him? She would lose her voice. Had Mr K. desired her in a fleeting embrace? She felt nauseated.

Lacan realized the impasse Freud got himself into. If femininity has to remain only a mythical secret in Dora's precious jewel case, if no woman responds to Freud's invitation, then, it is true, there is no woman who can respond to man's sexuality if not as the 'nothing' that Mrs K. and Dora's mother were for their husbands, the 'nothing' which echoes Dora's question: what is it to be a woman? All femininity could just be the game of the girl behind the veil, in order to find a husband, just a perforated sheet, slightly open curtains, or the very clothes which cover women up, their masquerade. This was Lacan's challenge, which, of course, awaited a reply.

Here we are back at the questioning: the woman is put in question by Lacan, arrogantly, as only a man can. But authentic questions are never sweet; the embarrassing questions of children are often cruel. Let us grasp then this opportunity for the silent and the incomprehensible to respond to the questioning challenge: that is, if she does not speak and does not represent herself, she does not exist.

Against this provocative 'You do not exist, do you?', women from several corners of the world have raised their protests, each of them starting to say something. They were called to speak to defend their very existence; from a position of object they were pushed into the position of subjects, thanks to a brutal questioning of their existence. But it is this very questioning (of sexual difference, in this case) which makes them subjects who have to answer for their existence to the other. The Lacanian arrogance provokes women into speech; by barring femininity from a universal, the sheet which hides women away, it makes each of us try to tell, each in a different way, what is the Woman which no woman is entirely. If there is 'Woman' that must be silence: the silence of what has not been touched by the contamination of language; that is, unsplit, asexual. Words seem to stop in front of this w-hole that women sexually represent to un-mask the illusion of a wholeness that language offers. The architec-ture of language, like the contours of shadows, has an empty centre; whether you want to call it 'non-illusion' or 'truth', whether you want to call it 'nothing' or 'something', this hole is encountered in speech in the form of its limits: an interruption or an interference in the flow of our words. Hysteria speaks this conflict within language by saying 'nothing'. Men, in different ways, are no more spared this conflict with language; the unconscious is 'unisex'.

What does 'The Woman does not exist' mean, then? For Lacan the order of words is the order of things, existence is what human beings conceive as existent, and we know that for Lacan human beings are defined by the fact that they speak, that they are im-mersed in language. Existence is what language considers as such; language selects and names existence. Language represses, or in more dramatic terms kills, the thing in favour of a representative; it represents the things of the world but is not them, or rather it is a world of its own. The question then is: does the woman exist in this world or, rather, in this symbolic order in any position aside from that of object, however precious? Is she not precisely what is repressed by language? Repression to which women are no less subjected than men, for they speak too.

The bet of several women, especially analysts, is that if the un-conscious can be allowed to speak (that is, exist) by psychoanalysis, so can the woman. Freud discovered the unconscious thanks to the hysterics who talked to Breuer and himself; Breuer's patient Anna O. called it the 'talking cure'. Psychoanalysis started with listening seriously to the talk of women. In 'Studies on hysteria' (Breuer and Freud, 1893), Freud had to expend a few words to justify why the object of his scientific work was women's chat and amorous intrigues. Of course women who speak do not reveal or make the Woman exist; they make women exist, and women can say a lot about what does not exist. They could tell Freud the unconscious because, like a symptom, a woman is closer to it: she is the symptom of man, but, now after psychoanalysis, 'she' is the unconscious which speaks. From being the symptom, the woman who speaks reveals something of this woman who does not exist in language if not, either veiled or denigrated or as a pain in the neck, as a symptom indeed. The tight, even though conflictual and ambivalent, bond between feminism and psychoanalysis could be explained by this more radical bond between the suffering of the symptom and its cure. Hysteria is the place where women present themselves as symptomatic, *en souffrance*, burdened by a mystery which concerns all of us, men and women.

Always like vestals, women have been entrusted with a burning fire, whose secrets they themselves do not know; they just enact and represent them. Think of hysterical scenarios: the hunting and burning of witches for their dealings with magic or evil in the Middle Ages (nowadays we tolerate them by calling them psychic). Or you have to look at the way *les grandes hystériques* of the Selpetrière hospital were seen and photographed in their enraptured communications with a mysterious absence (Didi-Huberman, 1982); or at our capricious and seductive Lolitas, the adolescent at the mercy of lunar influences, so desirable and so puzzling when a sudden hysterical fit enacts pain and suffering. As they are usually only passing fits with no serious consequence, then one allows them to fall within the mode of the comedy *dell'arte*. But art speaks there where the verbal expression finds its limits, against which it remains without echoes.

Art, like the hysterical symptom, stands out only through the cut of finely embroidered curtains, in a framed picture or within the written page. Hysteria is associated with comedy as it claims pain in parts of the body which are medically perfectly healthy; psychiatry is wary of hysterics as one is wary of a liar. Freud called this phenomenon conversion of mental pain into the body. The hysteric's soul takes possession of her body. Who is lying, the body or the soul? They are both telling the truth, the truth of their conflict, the paradoxical solution of two orders of things converging in the body of the woman: the encounter–clash of the symbolic and of the 'real'.

Why comedy, though? Could we not see it as the enactment of a tragedy instead, even though with a tinge of humour or of truthful mockery?

The mockery of tragedy is comedy, a distance taken from it. Tragedy is not an enactment in itself, as it aims at unveiling a catastrophic truth. The final swift and radically destructive action in Greek tragedy is the precipitation of a long preparation for it, in so far as the tragic sense derives from an attempt to keep at bay the ineluctable. Tragedy can have a cathartic function. It can protect you from your nightmares by actually showing them to you. It shows you the ones closest to yours; in fact it enacts our most universal myths: Oedipus, King Lear, Hamlet and so on. It leads to an original and final catastrophe. It uncovers and unfolds in front of us our most rooted and dreaded fears. Tragedy is what lies always behind the obsessional armour rather than the hysterical embroidery. Obsessionality could be compared to an endless rehearsal for the final catastrophe, without it ever being allowed to take place. The lie of the obsessional is more radical, as s/he does not take a distance from his/her imaginary catastrophic truth: s/he is at war with it.

Comedy seems to be the only bearable way to represent a tragedy. It is the crack in the armour, something women come to represent through their bleeding vagina, a shameful revelation: the armour bleeds. In comedy, tragedy takes on the form of a reassuring jest. The *lazzo* of the *commedia dell'arte*,[2] like the Freudian *'witz'* ('Joke': see Freud, 1905c), releases a revelation only by transforming it into a joke; maybe our laughter is always bitter laughter!

Consider the *lazzo* of 'the fly': the mime chases the buzzing of an invisible fly with the most delirious pirouettes. Finally when he catches it he will slowly tear off its invisible wings and gobble it up with complete satisfaction. All this will not go without consequences: the scoundrel suddenly starts to jolt about in ridiculous distress, with a violent final landing on the floor. Then you know that the fly is finally dead and digested. All's well that ends well! Whether we find it comic or not, the hysterical symptom, like the Italian jest, has nevertheless shown the suffering, the tear, Pierrot's tear, the drop on the cheek of the clown's mask. Greek tragedy too could only take place under the actors' thick masks. Tragedy can take place only with a hysterical mediation; it needs a screen. Art is born out of a hysterical mediation; from its essence of comedy art can step towards its other forms.

Psychoanalysis, too, was born out of Freud's encounter with hysterical symptoms, from which he developed his art. And Lacan took this point up when he said that the primary aim of psychoanalysis is to hysterisize the analysand, as that is the first step towards the form of art proper to psychoanalysis, the art of language.

The analyst is supposed to speak well. Fine speech in psychoanalysis is not rhetorical or embroidered speech but revelatory, true speech. Language is something you cannot abuse; Wittgenstein thought that if you do not use it well it will throw you into confusion and darkness. The access to this art, like all art, is not dictated by already made formulas representing specific contents of the mind; it rather follows the laws by which language makes the unconscious speak; language is always a hysterical dramatization, always a cover and a search for the expression of the inexpressible. The analyst attempts a dialogue with the unconscious as that leftover which language cannot help revealing in its gaps, its moments of failure and contradiction.

Therefore hysteria opened up the unconscious to psychoanalysis. It did so because hysteria is based not so much on a failure of language as on a disagreement with the father's language, in which the woman's body speaks the disagreement. The body joins in the conversation. Both hysteria and psychoanalysis deal with the borders of language, but they do so while standing on different sides: the hysteric resorts to the body to express her disagreement, the analyst reconverts the disagreement into the body of language. Hysteria stops at this conflict, in an endless war without winners and without losers: for a revelation constantly denies itself. Hysteria is not artistic expression in itself, rather its embryo. In its pathological forms it can function, on the contrary, as a brake to further forms of production. Like psychoanalysis it does not produce anything, as it is only a possibility of production. Without art and without analysis, hysteria can only produce symptoms. Its encounter with the analytical discourse does not produce art. But it may produce a cure.

Most readers will know of the case of Mary Barnes and her

journey through madness as she described it in a book together with her therapist Joseph Berke (Barnes and Berke, 1971). Whatever the clinical label, schizophrenia, hysteria or obsessional neurosis, I am concerned with her journey, as she herself called it. Journey indicates here movement, change, a falling and re-emerging which no clinical label can immobilize. In her book, her journey starts from the beginning of her life and goes all the way through to her healing breakdown in the Community of Kingsley Hall in London.

Her psychotic breakdown follows an intermingling of hysterical and obsessional characteristics in her familiar and emotional background. Mental hospitals could not do much for her catatonic states, which she expressed in the form of a hard shell under which she was getting 'buried and buried'. She could not break through it because it was like 'brittle ice' enveloping the whole family, and if the ice broke they would all be drowned; a slight movement could have been fatal.

This family obsessional enclosure had a leak via Mary and, more precisely, through her anus. Since she was a little girl she had secretly found a hole in this all-enveloping shell: through the anus she could penetrate herself with her fingers and play with her own excrement inside and outside herself. She moulded it and kept it stuck under her mattress: this was her first painting. Later, in her going-down journey at Kingsley Hall, she covered herself with excrement: Mary and her shit were one and the same thing. Her excremental product enveloped her. There was no separation between herself and her own representation, between the surface of her body and her inside. As in hysteria, the work of art and the artist merged in one body. In order to stop this trapping circularity of her body, Mary stopped eating and defecating; nothing had to come in and nothing could go out. She made of her body a static, almost dead body. She had to abandon it in order to be able to represent it by other means, it was a farewell, and not a death. Like Lefort's wolf-child, she had to bear her body empty.

Maybe it was an enactment of death in the way that an actor can die every evening on stage in order to resurrect and die again the next evening. In order to overcome her anality she had to explode with her madness, and among her ruins she found her resurrection. And when her excrement started to shape biblical representations, they became art. Her therapist offered her paint in place of shit, and Mary became an artist. The hysterical virginal illusion was thus overcome. She did not emerge whole from her journey. On the contrary, her body had to be left at the mercy of her anger, desire and emptiness. She called it the 'It', the thing. She met this 'It' in its diabolic, psychotic form. I am not sure about her psychotic structure as I do not see a delusional system in her. I would rather see her delusional phenomena as the hysterical horizon of madness. Kingsley Hall and its philosophy allowed her to experience the unbearable rawness of psychosis only as a journey (and not as a state of being). She gave her journey a meaning, her authentic quest for truth which was her faith. She had faith both in the therapist and in God and this gave a meaning to her experience, and even to her possibly psychotic structure. It mediated it and made it bearable. She started to paint in the Name of the Father which for her was God, and she identified with Christ. So Mary Barnes's psychosis was provided with a means of communication through art. A meaning mediated her psychotic experience, functioned as a safety net for the plunge into the unfillable hole of the 'real', that very hole which feminine sexuality seems to represent.

The limit between a *délire mystique* and an authentic mysticism is thin, but a difference there is; we do not say that Saint Teresa of Avila or contemplative monks are mad, while people like President Schreber, even when his delusions concern a theological system, we do not believe. The latter cannot invoke a witness in their favour, as their gods are persecuting gods. And because of this lack of a guarantor who gives meaning to their experience, they are visited by senseless gods and condemned to the most total solitude.

The libido is only masculine, Freud thought, and not wrongly, because if there is a feminine sexuality it is not of the order of libido but of the order of the void. If libido evokes the experience of ejaculating energy, the void evokes a contemplative experience, closer to a mystical one indeed, but, like psychosis, it is an experience without divine guarantee and therefore rarely experienced in its pure form; the *jouissance* of the woman can take place only behind a symbol which can guarantee it. The woman who is encountered in the symbolic order is a woman, the earthly woman.

5

Compliance and Disagreement

A train arrives at a station. A little boy and a little girl, brother and
sister, are seated in a compartment face to face next to the window
through which the building along the station platform can be seen
passing as the train pulls to a stop. 'Look', says the brother, 'we're at
Ladies!'. 'Idiot!', replies his sister, 'Can't you see we're at Gentlemen?'.... For these children, Ladies and Gentlemen will be hence-
forth two countries towards which each of their souls will strive on
divergent wings, and between which a truce will be more impossible
since they are actually the same country and neither can compromise
on its own superiority without detracting from the glory of the other.
(Lacan, 1977a, p. 152)

Thus Lacan's illustration of a childhood memory awoken in a friend
by one of Lacan's diagrams: toilet doors, two identical doors above
which you can read their difference, Ladies and Gentlemen.

Evocation recalls evocation, which in psychoanalysis is called
free association, so that this illustration awoke in me another one: a
joke I heard as a child. Two babies are in a cradle. 'I am a boy', one
says to the other, 'and you?' 'I don't know', answers the other. 'Don't
you? Let me pull off your blanket and tell you then.' 'No, I am
ashamed.' 'Come on, don't you want to know if you are a boy or a
girl?' At last the other baby gives in and lets the blanket be pulled off
by the boy, who exclaims: 'You are a girl, you've got pink knickers!'

I cannot remember my reaction to the joke as a child, but certainly
I bore it in my mind, although I remembered it only on this occasion. I must have smiled and dismissed the joke then. But now I
cannot help finding in both jokes a relevance which goes beyond the
smile, however knowing, which they elicit. Jokes, fairy tales, popu-

lar stories, myths, even superstitions are metaphors which describe a world in a rigorous way.

A joke makes you laugh as a relief from a previous tension caused by unpalatable truths. In the case in question you wonder what the baby is going to say; it elicits an expectation and a fear of a revelation. Can you imagine if the baby really shouted out what was expected? But the relief! The baby could already, like us, only recognize the standards, the clothings, of a difference. And hence the laughter: how funny, how stupid to take the veil for what lies behind it! Not even a baby can reveal what originally lies there, before we veil and dress it up; it is not by chance that babies cannot speak. What lies behind the colours of our sexual teams, then? I would have liked the joke to tell me but, like those two babies, I cannot say it.

As soon as we can say something we can only distinguish doorplates on public toilets, which indicate the law of urinary segregation. One could object that the girl had a knowledge of a difference, otherwise she would not have complied with the boy and would not have felt ashamed. She certainly knew the words 'boy' and 'girl', but until her sexual enlightenment at the hands of her friend, she did not even know that it was under the blanket that she had to look for her sex. Now she thinks she knows because another has told her. But could she not believe him and look for it herself? Even so she would have only followed the other's instructions, as she would not have known what her difference in relation to another was. She would have presumably felt complete in that respect.

All she knows after the joke, which was not such for her and which I am managing to spoil so well for everybody else, is that her world must be pink, although it might not feel that pink to her. In the same way we do not recognize the king by looking for his identity under his clothes but, on the contrary, his royal bearing and his standards tell us he is one, even if he is Anderson's naked king.[1]

So she knows now that she is a girl, but only behind pink knickers, that's for sure! Knickers to offer to the eyes of the boy. We could see here illustrated the core of both pornographic and fetishist excitement, phenomena which probably share something of the nature and the mechanism of a joke.

Why cannot we, grown-ups in the know, pull off the veil and shout out what is there? If somebody wants to do so I challenge them to do so, but it is unlikely s/he can say more than words, that is, than veils, unless this person wishes to be indecent or shock us with bad language, by making either an exhibitionist or a fool of her/himself. One can do it, but only at the cost of a scandal. Still, is sex not the star of the moment? Is it not tackled, taught, theorized and even encouraged by all areas of knowledge and practice in our culture?[2] We know a lot about sex; it seems that the silence and the interdictions which have bottled up sexuality for centuries have now popped like champagne corks. Foucault thought that all societies of all times devise certain mechanisms of sexuality (1976–84). Today our device of sexuality is to talk a lot about sex; we talk about what centuries of sex have kept mostly to themselves: we talk to the doctor, to all types of counsellor and therapist, to acupuncturists, to homeopaths, on radio programmes, in court if we have to divorce or are homosexual or have been raped, and no types of book, from fiction to philosophy, spare it; and of course, last but not least, in psychoanalysis. They all know or want to know about our sexuality, whether we like it or not. We have to acknowledge that there is sex; we have to put up with it. From tolerance to apology the step is a small one: not only can we not help being sexed, but sex is good for us. We must have sex, in one way or another. And here we have sexology, orgasm therapies, sexual antidotes to repression or to housewives' depression and so on. We have defeated the dirtiness of sexuality; we seem to have succeeded better than other times in controlling its indecency.

Sexuality is no longer governed by religious, legal or moral prescriptions but by a molecular and utter control (and information) over our sexual lives. Our morality is a basically hygienic one: we want to beat the dirt, to sterilize, kill viruses and germs. Like obsessive housewives we check, clean and get rid of any speck of dust deposited on our furniture.

As in the joke, it seems that the more we want to have sex in check, to come face to face with it, the more it escapes us. In wanting to tear apart the veils in the hope of coming to terms with a supposed truth about sexuality that might be free from cultural constructions and differences, we just lay bare the indifference. In wanting to come to the core of how and what a woman is, apart from cultural and historical determinations, we find no woman; but, I would add, no man either. What is this trick?

It is true we discover anatomical parts about which we know a lot and which we call by their proper names: vagina, penis, breasts, clitoris and so on. But as with our liver or circulation of the blood, they denote only our scientific knowledge of anatomy, not any sexual knowledge. As in medicine, whose knowledge is based on diseased bodily organs, all we know about sex is sex that is hurting or lacking.

It is still the fate of sex to be known in its negative forms. We really shut up or do not need to talk about it when it is 'successful'. All our sexual science is based on the unsuccessfulness of sex; we go to sex experts when it does not work. We speak and know about it so long as it does not work or, maybe, it does not work so long as we speak about it.

Foucault hinted at the possibility that our search for sexual knowledge and sexual techniques might have become another device of sexuality, an enjoyment in itself. But enjoyment itself cannot be expressed verbally, precisely because language is based on its failure. Language is, precisely, failed enjoyment; it is the veil, the clothes that cover and split sexuality. Freud said that the complexity of human sexuality depends on the fact that it is assumed only via its negation, that is, the threat of castration. Castration is inherent in the function of speech. Speech is itself a split out of the undifferentiation of the unnamed; it splits the child from the mother, the thing from its representation. We seem to assume our sexuality only at the cost of repressing and losing part of it. We need to castrate ourselves in order to make love: we cannot enjoy the whole. Language claims its own; yes, we enjoy the dance of the veils. We enjoy the masquerade of women and the parade of men; our desire is awoken by what lies mysteriously hidden behind.

What, after all, was revealed to a doctor at the end of the last century when dealing with hysterics and perverse people? Not misplaced uteruses or anatomical freaks but psyche, the soul. With Freud we witness the emergence of the soul in the very place which science had chosen as its object of study: the body. This body, which was being studied and defined by medicine, became to his ears a speaking body. The uteruses of hysterics, the body-woman, this bodily body, this neutral object which is not supposed to think or speak, left-over of the division operated by language; this body of the hysteric starts to speak and, stupefied, we say: it is lying! It is a comedy! If the body cannot speak it can become paralysed or have a fit. It plays the *commedia dell'arte*. And, of course, art, whether comedy or not, is supposed to say something, or more than something. Art, like the unconscious, pushes language to its own borders, it is an attempt to say more . . . not all, as we can deal only with the veils of the mystery of our existence. The soul is divided and is the effect of this division.

In the beginning was the word. The word carved and divided into forms the original chaos. Here is the myth of Genesis, of a God who operated a split on himself through his word of creation. How much easier it was when the gods explained everything, when both Aristophanes and the Bible could explain the incompleteness of the human condition as God's punishment for our arrogance. Maybe our democratic souls cannot accept any longer such tyrannical gods. It was at the democratic point that Freud's atheism gave a new name to this *deus ex machina*, the name of a pagan idol: the phallus.

At the beginning of this book, I gave a brief description of the Villa of the Mysteries in Pompeii as representing the mystery of sexuality in its feminine guise. This became clear on my first trip. Later, I went back to Pompeii, this time to visit the House of the Phallus where the cult of social power and prosperity was exercised. I knew that the sense of phallic wholeness had been preserved until our time. It was preserved and defended by denying entrance to women. Then, the House was closed for restoration. Shortly after its restoration, women were permitted to enter it. And I thought: yes, women can enter the 'House of the Phallus'. Women can now enter the house of social power and wholeness. So, what is happening to the psychoanalytic phallus as representative of sexual difference? As Juliet Mitchell (1975) has said, all human order has always been social, and the power of the phallus has always coincided with the human order to which women have been submitted as the other of the phallus. In fact, power implies the subjection of another. Power participates in the logics of separation and castration.

But what is this male power over women? In the unconscious there is no such myth as a war in which women lost their freedom. Women are not a social class or a minority in the human world. Had they asked for their right of equality, who could have ignored them? But they never seem to obtain that specific right, even when it is explicitly stated in the declaration of human rights. It is as if, even under the most progressive civil codes, women obey another law: an intimation to submit. Not by chance, feminism has turned its attention from its earlier social rights vindications towards more subjective struggles and theoretical analysis regarding a submission which goes beyond its legal abolition. 'Submission' as a signifier imposes its own law on women. It is not at the level of pagan myths that the feminine signifier lies trapped. On the contrary, their rites (the sacrifices and the whippings) are rites of purification and of passage, in order to become Domina; a mistress (plates 7 and 1). She is in both the Dionysiac and Apolline tradition, the minister of the gods.

Pagan sexual difference is based on the phallic difference where both men and women have to integrate it through rites of passage, whereas in biblical monotheism the phallus becomes the golden idol, the false law of the golden calf. The Name of the Father found the Muslim–Judaeo-Christian unconscious as the law of submission and of penance because of Eve's prohibited act. She gave us birth at the cost of the Garden of Eden. Her biblical responsibility for human misery weighs on her, as well as on men who act on this responsibility. The father as the possessor of the phallus cannot be easily integrated. Unlike Dionysus, the monotheist god requires the submission of women as the result of their 'initiation'. Freud knew it very well when he thought that to become a woman is a very twisted and exhausting business. Monotheism is in fact the religion of the One, whole omnipotent god. This god does not lack anything, does not allow difference. The Christian woman is left without her own earthly initiation rites, except, as we have already pointed out, in the mystical choice.[3]

Simone de Beauvoir's protestations about woman being abused by man are not all that coherent, since they claim both a noble weakness in the woman, that is, her difference, and her right to be powerful like a man. She is different but she should not be other. De Beauvoir (1972) claims women are different but then calls that difference inauthentic and forced on them. Yet is this incoherence not what all feminist theorists are trying to unravel and explain? Others explain it in deterministic or materialistic terms: the phallic system has been declared bankrupt; it is no longer needed either historically or economically. Feminism is what emerges when the doors in the House of the Phallus remain ajar.

Psychoanalysis too has always been in difficulties when it wants to define sexual difference. Whatever bias it takes, whether an intrinsic one or a constructed one,[4] psychoanalysis cannot look at it if not as an unconscious difference. Not because there is such a thing as a feminine unconscious, but because *this difference is the unconscious itself.* It was with the hysterics' 'No' to the phallic logic that Freud discovered the non-conscious, indeed the unconscious. We could say that *the unconscious is feminine,* it is the negation, the un-, the other, of phallic consciousness. Therefore, in spite of the doors left ajar, there is a difference; the phallic whole image leaves a residue – the other exists. Certainly it is only to be more or less subtly repressed and subjected. Nevertheless it was the discovery of the unconscious that subverted the value of a supremacy of the master ego over other visions of the world. This is like the Roman armies which conquered the highly sophisticated civilization of ancient Greece, only to adopt and spread that civilization over their half-worldwide empire. From the Roman perspective of power and strength the Greeks were irremediably losers, whereas from a historical perspective we appreciate the Greek superiority. Psychoanalysis subverts the supremacy of the master precisely because it has discovered, through the speaking woman, other supremacies and other discourses. And to a psychoanalyst the power of our *conscious* knowledge appears with blind attributes of ignorance and misrecognition.

The problem is that to speak is already a phallic function: the woman, by speaking, implicitly reiterates her own subjection. This is the paradox of the woman, whose paradigm is well illustrated by the case of the well-educated and articulate Dora (Freud, 1905a),[5] who, through her illness, chose to speak by means of her 'ignorant' body. Her identification with the symbolic order of the father, her speech, went on strike, as it were. But strike does not mean non-work or non-language. On the contrary, like a workers' strike, it is the expression of the highest degree of a worker's consciousness. It is this division between her own words and the impossibility of uttering them without losing her specific 'otherness' that psychoanalysis has detected in the anti-discourse of hysterical women. The hysterical discourse is the discourse not only of the woman but of the artist, of the mystic, of minorities; in other words, of the other. The specific instance of the woman, whether she identifies or not with her otherness, is as a subject who can participate in two forms of life. I mean here at least the two basic forms of life of compliance and disagreement. Like artistic communication, which has to use the words that ordinary language offers in order to use them differently or even subvert them, Dora's illness was the effect of her compliance, even identification and complicity with the world of her father, and her disagreement with the place it assigned to her. With her aphonia she was on strike for the recognition of the difference which would give her the right to speak. Hysteria is, and has been in the past, the effect of the woman who wants to speak and who, in so doing, risks losing her soul.

We could say that if the phallus threatens men with losing their penis, it threatens the woman with losing her 'feminine' soul. But the soul resorted to by psychoanalysis is this very loss of itself. Not even a woman can reveal it from under her alluring dress. She can represent its symptom, its possibility as well as its impossibility, the incoherence of the soul, its division. The woman, like the unconscious, is not ontological but ethical. Maybe it was easier to be a woman when she had her well-defined realm, her seat in Lacan's train, and enjoyed as well as suffered the silence of her almost absolute Otherness, with no ethical biblical choices to make.

President Schreber's delusional system describes well, in a psychotic form, the feminine signifiers. Having been turned into a woman, Schreber submitted 'his/her' body to the voluptuousness of God's rays for the benefit of a new human race to be procreated through his woman's body.

Women now can know, and are trying to articulate what they might know of, this sinful *jouissance*. Or they might know as little as the boy in the cradle. I can see in my practice how hard it is for the woman to say what she is; sometimes women come to analysis only to try to say it. Some have reached the top floor of the House of the Phallus only to fade away in their anorexia; in the limelight of success some faint, just like a woman. Or like a character that was popular in a TV serial of several years ago, a black journalist who had reached a privileged position in a white society and who could have transcended his black destiny. But he was not able to transcend it, he was looking for his roots, for his original culture with its values and truths. He was in fact looking for another vision of the world, for the 'other' that he did not have to be but that he chose to be.

6

The Paradoxes of the Earthly Woman

Freud's studies on hysteria

Psychoanalysis started with the treatment of hysterical patients by way of hypnosis. The latter helped them to remember and go back to the traumatic events at the supposed roots of their symptoms. In fact from the earlier descriptions of hypnotic treatment made by Breuer and Freud in 'Studies on hysteria' (1893), they seem to have found very little resistance, as the hysterical symptoms appeared easily altered by the hypnotic 'transference'.[1] The patients, mainly women, seemed to respond promptly to the appeal of love which transference always involves. The way psychoanalysis was born out of hypnosis was a two-way rejection of hypnosis: the reticence of his hysterical patients to be hypnotized matched Freud's resistance to and clumsiness in exerting it.

Psychoanalysis proper arose from the limits of hypnosis as suggestion. With Frau Emmy von N., Freud was still trying to 'suggest' her memories away. We could say that Freud, after Bernheim's experiments, put a stress on the role of suggestion in hypnosis. The invention of psychoanalysis was the effect of Freud's attempts to circumvent the power of suggestion. This is the power that the analyst receives from the patient as the 'one supposed to know'.

With the suggestion technique Freud poses himself half-way between hypnosis and consciousness. Psychoanalysis starts precisely within this interval between a state of consciousness and a state of hypnotic suggestion at the hands of the Other. It is in this gap between the ego and the Other that the unconscious appears and psychoanalysis keeps finding it.

In Dora's treatment Freud had already given up hypnosis, making a definite step into the psychoanalytic method proper, characterized by a change of the patient's position in relation to the therapist: the patient is no longer subjected to the power of hypnosis via the gaze but is asked to speak freely. Yet we can see in Dora's case that when she was offered this possibility she stubbornly refused it. When Dora was given a choice, she could, unlike the earlier cases, choose to resist. Freud discovered the mechanism of resistance from this apparent paradox of a reversal from subjection to the Other's power to its rejection, which was more clearly revealed by the giving up of hypnotic power. Thereby Freud made resistance the motor of his method rather than hypnosis, but not before he discovered the importance of transference, as a negative one, in Dora's resistance. Only at this point did he realize a relation between resistance to analysis and his patient's leitmotif of an early traumatic seduction and the resistance to admitting it. So resistance put Freud on the path of sexuality, which was, at the time, still considered as genitality.

Sexuality and seduction

Nineteenth-century psychiatry of the time held the traditional view of hysteria as a particular kind of sexual demand, a uterine lack of balance indeed. Thereupon the hysteric needed a virile husband who could calm her down. Freud takes it on from there. Behind most of his patients' stories there was an early seduction generally perpetrated by their own fathers, disguised in the Freudian early text on hysteria as uncles. A sexual trauma was always lurking behind the hysteric *belle indifference*, and the same desire for revenge which we will examine in Dora's case is coveted by Frau Emmy and Fraulein Elisabeth von R. In contrast to practitioners of medicine and psychiatry, Freud did not pretend he knew something about them: that they needed a good fuck or a hot bath. But Freud's realization was that whereas his probing aimed at wanting to know something about his patients' sexuality, he had to wrestle with what they already knew but would not say.

What then was this that they did not want to know about their sexuality? Was it a sexual desire or a sexual trauma lurking behind

Plate 1   Domina, the matron of the house where the rites of the
mysteries took place

Plate 2   Child reading the sacred text to the veiled initiate under
the guidance of the initiated matron/mother

Plate 3   Unveiling and veiling of the sacrifice, and Silenus
playing the lyre

Plate 4   Pan's woman suckling a goat, and the terrified woman

Plate 5   Satyr holding up the monstrous mask reflected in the cup
of Silenus' divination and the sacred couple, Dionysus and
Ariadne

Plate 6   The unveiling of the phallus and the demon of shame

Plate 7   Woman flagellated by the demon of shame, and the
dancing Bacchant

Plate 8   The dressing of the Dionysiac bride

the indifference? The puzzle about feminine sexuality starts here. What is this nucleus which evades memory and consciousness? What is the 'cause' of hysterics getting ill from reminiscences? Freud probed into the 'empty space' of feminine sexuality, but he missed it. His investigations of hysterics' sexuality led him always to the same rock: the notion of sexual trauma. Having found that in almost all cases his patients had been seduced as children, Freud did not know what to believe; either that all of his patients coming from well-to-do and respectable families had been sexually abused by their parents or other relatives, or that the very encounter with male sexuality constituted an abuse for the hysteric, a trauma indeed. He could not believe either. He believed the first hypothesis but it was not sufficient. But he could not believe that sexuality as such is traumatic, either, as he was holding fast to his conviction that girls are made for boys and boys for girls. Is there something beyond genitality in sex, then? It was this question that led Freud to discover infantile and childhood sexuality, the pre-genital. But as we have seen, his investigations ended in the conclusion that there is only one libido, and it is masculine.

We had to wait for Lacan to discover that there is sexuality beyond the one masculine libido, that there is 'more' than one *jouissance*, or enjoyment, that there is the 'other one'. Freud saw it on the face of Elisabeth von R., as when

> if one pressed and pinched the hyperalgesic skin and muscles of her legs, her face assumed a peculiar expression which was one of pleasure rather than pain. She cried out – and I could not help thinking that it was as though she was having a voluptuous tickling sensation – her face flushed, she threw back her head and shut her eyes and her body bent backwards. None of this was very exaggerated but it was distinctly noticeable and it could only be reconciled with the view that her disorder was hysterical and that the stimulation had touched upon a hysterogenic zone. (Breuer and Freud, 1893, p. 137)

Gropingly he sought to uncover the cause of such a voluptuousness, but he could not recognize it as 'other'. And Freud's misrecognition in the face of his own discoveries can be used as the key to his analytic relation to Dora. I have assumed that readers know something, perhaps a lot, about this famous case. But I will now discuss it in detail.

Dora

When asked to talk, Dora could not reveal her secret; something was missing in her words. Freud was faced with an incompatibility between sexual desire and words. But Freud assumed that whatever was missing in her own story was demanding recognition through her hysterical symptoms, that something was striving for recognition. His theory that hysterical symptoms were related to sexuality was confirmed by the amorous intrigues which seemed to entangle all the characters, Freud included, in a fishing net. Something about sexuality could not be spoken about, but it was the patient who was showing the marks on her body. I said 'something about sexuality' and not sexuality in itself for, as we have already said, we do not know what sexuality is. It can never be grasped in its pure form. We can only grasp its effects on the person who is experiencing it. But this was the problem Freud stumbled on. His theory of sexuality at that point clashed with Dora's reactions. He had not yet distinguished sexuality as a purely biological factor from its conflictual effects on and in the human being. The human being is for Lacan the one who speaks, but speaking is not knowing. Dora knew a lot about sex through books and encyclopaedias: in fact her knowledge was considered a form of sexual obsession. But this kind of knowledge did not seem to correspond to the kind of sexuality enacted in her body and revealed through her hysterical symptoms.

This clash between two kinds of knowledge is well represented by the clash which took place between Freud and Dora. It was this fragment of failed analysis which Freud chose to discuss at great length as a lesson to be learned, as a warning to the psychoanalyst against his own supposed knowledge of things. He can do no more than witness the impossibility of speaking sexuality in the silence into which the failing word plunges. The analytic discourse keeps bumping into an empty space, the area excluded by language. The analyst is faced with a resistance, the silence of a secret, a knowledge not to be spoken about and therefore not known (a *savoir* which cannot be *connu*).

Resistance emerged more and more as the question of love was pushed by Freud. He tried to convince Dora that, as a woman, she had to love a man. But Dora had not assumed her body as feminine or as a sexed body at all. Her body was possessed by this refusal. It started to speak of its own accord, but Dora was not in accord with it. She could not agree with Freud. She did not agree with her body. And this lack of agreement with anything is the hysterical drama through which Freud discovered the unconscious itself. The unconscious reveals a 'No', a radical discord between different levels of truth. We can see how the hysterical symptoms inscribe painful truths, how the body becomes a battlefield where denials and revelations fight their war.

A discourse, in the Lacanian sense, is nothing else but the specific ethical position we take within that network of symbolic agreements which is language. We are pinned down into an 'overdetermined' position to be either accepted or questioned. The unconscious belongs to us, therefore, so long as we can agree or not with something, say yes or no.

The body and the mirror stage

Freud could listen to the discourse of the hysteric's body so far as it 'joined in the conversation' with all its ambiguity of sense, and he would challenge it in the conversation. The symptom is painful because it betrays in a skewed fashion what you came to believe as your ethical settlement, your constituted rigid truths. It disrupts the compromise one has with oneself.

Dora admitted the existence of a betrayal, but only as something done by the others: she was betrayed by her mother, father, by Mr and Mrs K. Only from looking out could she see her own betrayal of herself. She did not want to love or make love to Mr K., she did not want her father to make love to Mrs K., and she did not want to love Freud and could not accept his excessive love for 'her' truth. And it is true that Freud's interpretations aimed at unmasking that she lied too, and that all her symptoms were telling him that she passionately loved her father, Mr K. and even himself. But it was too true for Dora, too arrogantly true to mean anything. The love Freud was talking about did not take Dora's conflict with it into account.

After all, we all love and want to be loved, and Freud realized only a moment too late that she loved so much that she identified with the objects of her love while refusing to be an object of their love. So her love had no objects; her symptoms betray exactly this transcendence, this platonic love. But Dora is not Socrates, she does not accept this philosophical transcendence which nevertheless underlined her symptoms. In fact she had abolished the real objects of desire only to love their images or pictures like the Virgin and her beauty, the beauty of Mrs K. And Freud was wrong again when he later identified in Mrs K. Dora's object of love, because she loved Mrs K. not as an object but as the ideal image of herself, that is, the mystery of her sex and of her own sexual desire. Mrs K., like Dora's mother, refused the role of Domina (initiation into womanhood) which Dora was desperately expecting of her. Hysteria is enlightening on how feminine rites of initiation are conspicuously missing. Dora's feminine body was an image outside herself, left out and not integrated into the image she had of herself; that is, her ego-image. Unlike Diotima, Dora does not progress from lower objects towards higher ideal ones. Diotima was, for Socrates, his active feminine knowledge. Socrates in being initiated by a woman only follows his pagan culture. Dora, like Socrates, is in love with this mysterious feminine knowledge but she has not symbolically been initiated into it.

At this point, it is important to remind oneself of Lacan's Mirror Stage, as the stage constitutive of the ego of the subject. We fall in love with an image of ourselves which is outside ourselves, as when a baby recognizes him/herself for the first time in the image reflected in the mirror. After all the image is always outside, as it is a reflection to the eyes of the subject. The ego is just an image, but it is an image into which we alienate and split our being. But, of course, the image we assume in the mirror is an ideal image, as when the baby, still lacking the mastery of his/her body which cannot as yet stand up, welcomes with jubilation his/her reflected new image of him/herself, which is supported and held by a mother or any other supporter; that is, which is completed by another. In order to assume our image in the mirror we require it to be already there in the Other. Winnicott identified the mother as the baby's mirror; Lacan saw the mirror as her gaze. We are images as long as we are objects of another's gaze, and consequently of all the expectations, desire, determinations implied in it (plate 8).

All human things concur to make up our human specific image. We have only to recognize, accept or refuse this image offered to us. To refuse it is not easy. This is the image Narcissus fell in love with;

this is the image of the completeness of the child held by another in front of the mirror, the Madonna with Child. If love is always narcissistic, nevertheless the other is the founding part of our narcissistic image. If we love ourselves, nevertheless it is only as other, before the mirror. It is in the pupil of the other that we see ourselves, in its gaze. After the separation from the other's face which the mirror achieves, the other's gaze is on our face; we are identified with our mirror's upholders (plate 8).

In Dora's case the maternal figure had withdrawn into darkness instead. Her image did not have a function of feminine identification for her. The mother was the one who, like Mrs K., did not give anything to her husband and her children. She appears as a lacking figure representing sexual refusal. With her housewife's obsessions, she cleaned up femininity, and made it unusable, especially for Dora, who could not use her mother's body as a specular support for her own feminine image. All Dora's conversion symptoms expressed an infantile fragmentation of her feminine body.

In the meantime, as her first dream showed, another figure came to save her life from burning urine – fire and water represent well the primitive elements of our infantile experience and phantasies of the body. This was the figure of the father.

The father

The male figure appears in the dream as one offering a support for Dora's identity. The mother's breast was replaced in her screen memory by her own thumb-sucking. But this narcissistic self-enclosure needed support from the other. In her case the support was represented by her brother's ear, which she pulled while sucking her own thumb. The screen image represented Dora's partial identification with a male figure: her little brother whose little ear is only a support from outside for her self-satisfaction. Her mirror image is supported by a male figure but a belittled one. The penis had not completely replaced the absence of the maternal insignia; that is, Dora could identify with a male figure so long as it was impotent, childlike or like her supposedly syphilitic father. A castrated man comes to represent the lack of the maternal image. The maternal body was not reflected in Dora's specular ego-image but had become a lost object, exiled from her, and femininity had become her secret love, so secret that even Freud was at great pains to reveal it.

Knowledge

However, maternity and femininity were also her secret knowledge, we might say, the secret about her sexuality held and trapped in her body. Freud constantly wondered where her sexual knowledge came from, and in the end he had an insight: it came from Mrs K. and, earlier on, from her governess. Which knowledge, though? Dora knew a lot, too much perhaps, about her father's venereal disease and about fellatio. She had a culture of the penis, but she was a virgin. The woman appeared in this culture as a negation, an absence of knowledge; her sexual enjoyment shines forth because of its absence. This is Dora's secret love for her mother's ungraspable enjoyment, ungraspable because in no symbolic framework for her, but in a *secret* (and not a *mystery*). There were no initiatory rites to do with a feminine symbolic identification.

The phallus

Was Freud then completely wrong in his interpretation about her love for father? We could suspect that if maternity was her repressed and then secret knowledge, paternity had to be the enigma of her own precarious identity. If maternity was something belonging to the *real* order, that is, to a level of existence which had not been symbolized, paternity was the support for her knowledge of the world. But, as we have already seen, this she had only partially assumed. Father represents for her a symbolic world where her position is 'nothing' for him,[2] as Mr K. put it during the scene on the lake. He represents a world where she can be symbolized either as object or as nothing. What is it to be a woman? This the father does not know.

Here we can see the phallic function in its full operation. The father has taken over and kept in darkness the function of the mother, so that he becomes the representative of the visible world. He dominates the previous darkness of the mother's womb.[3] Therefore he knows everything but the woman; he knows anything at the cost of not knowing her. Dora was then identifying with father so long as he symbolized her denied femininity, and so long as he was thought of as impotent, syphilitic, half blind and ill; that is, so long as his castration prevents him from 'knowing' the woman. His sexual 'means' and potency represented a threat to her sexual *in-difference*; it is in the hands of these two men's exchange that her symbolic position is exchanged too. In fact her encounter with Mr K.'s sexual desire turns upside down her enjoyment, derived from a world of pure asexual subjectivity, devoid of sexual objects, into one where she is in a pure position of object. So, in this world *à la belle âme*, we could say, there is no room for objects if not as 'pure' symbols; that is, symbols of the nothing which the woman symbolically is. Thereupon men too were not real objects of desire in their own right, and even less were their penises.

If the phallus was a symbol, then it could not exist as an object for Dora, whose unconscious seemed to draw the phallic point of view to its extreme logical consequences, almost to the point of mockery. The object, the 'real object' is not the one the symbolic order hands forward, or clandestinely offers in an embrace, as Freud suspected of Mr K., but the 'nothing' which the woman has and which cannot be offered. There is (a) 'no-thing'[4] which escapes men. They think they can exchange it but they miss it; they mistake her for it. This is the paradox of the object (a) which Dora secretly is but has not. We can articulate even further Dora's discourse, which could run like this: if the woman is an object of exchange and of desire for the phallic structure, thereafter I make of her an unusable object, like my mother's unusable domestic objects or like my mother herself. That meant that if the woman is an object value, she has to be loved for nothing and for not giving anything.

What appears peculiar in Dora, and in hysterical women in general, if not the fact that they passionately love *nothing*: neither this nor that? They might shelter under a masculine identification, but only to love the woman, the non-phallus or the lack of it. Dora loved, and wished men loved, the beauty which covers the woman's hole, this object which envelops an absence, an appearance of being and of completeness. A film director like Jean-Luc Godard, who attempted to discuss this issue in his film *Je vous salue, Marie*, shows the pregnant Virgin Mary offering the sight of her body to

Joseph's contemplation. But he could not touch or penetrate it; he had to worship it. And this untouchable nothing, the little object (a) for Lacan, is for Godard, as for Bataille, nothing less than God himself. When Mr K. said 'My wife is nothing for me' (or 'I do not get anything from her') Dora slapped him, and the slap meant 'That's why you should love her, and that's why I love her. Nothing is everything for me.'

For Dora, love did not come from desire for another sexed being: there was no symbolic difference between the two sexes. Love was constituted by mere images, photos and the undifferentiated exchange of presents. Desire is always denied by neurotics because it is frustrating and Dora did not want to know about this lack of something; she would rather have 'nothing'.

The virgin

But Dora's body enacted a delivery and sex as symptoms; this nothing hurts. The Virgin was the symbol of asexual fullness. Only the Virgin can deliver a child; the image of the Virgin is the total exclusion of the existence of sexual intercourse, the ideal image of feminine self-containment and sufficiency. Her creation is the fruit of God's direct contact with her. But this is already a step away from hysteria into the mystic vision of the world. But the problem of the hysteric is that she just misses that step, she only touches its borders.

Dora became a feminist symbol instead, and not by chance, as this case draws our attention to the fact that her body spoke feminine sexuality. She offers us a paradox, I would say the paradox of the earthly woman, and it is exactly in the earthly woman that mysticism and sexuality are implicated in a conflict without solution.

Why mysticism? Because this experience of the few has something structurally very close to the 'ideal' position of women, their complete voluntary subjection to God who compensates them by means of this mystical enjoyment. Their testimonies refer to a position of non-being; that is, as the object of God. They are absorbed in God's being. The mystics have renounced the enjoyment of earthly objects (neither this nor that) in order to yearn for the ultimate joy that only the supreme being can give. Mystics have, exactly like

Dora, renounced the phallic enjoyment, the earthly one, as it were. They are led by pure desire of the absolute, without the phallic mediation; that is, without a 'seeming' of being, without mirror alienation. The woman too has a difficult relation with the mirror, like the queen in Sleeping Beauty, who kept checking the integrity and fullness of her image, her beauty indeed, but only to be told by the mirror that she is not the most beautiful woman in her realm: there is always 'the other woman', who is. The mirror reflects what is lacking in the woman in order to be the most beautiful, in order to be whole. Women need the mirror exactly because they are not fully (*pas toute*, not-all) alienated in it, they have constantly to recompose their image, trying to hide under their make-up the hole which cannot be reflected in the mirror. Beauty is the feminine phallus as well as the dress of feminine modesty.

The opening, the breaking-up of the phallic image is the obscene. The obscene is the earthquake, the eruption, the exhibition of the void. When the Wolf-man's psychotic structure emerged in his second analysis his main symptom was his *idée fixe* namely, that he had a hole in his nose which he had to check all the time in his pocket mirror, and had to powder, just like a woman. Schreber too was placed in a feminine position in his delusional system. The difference with a woman is that her position is not delusional; she is placed in that position by the symbolic. *She is symbolically placed there*, in the 'real', beyond mirror and beyond words, beyond sight and beyond name, and her existence as a woman is determined by this symbolic placement in the 'real'. The 'real' to which women have access strips them of symbolic existence.[5] On the other hand, the mystic has placed herself fully in a feminine position. Via God she accedes to the 'real' of which an ecstatic 'enjoyment' is the effect. It is God himself who initiates her into her 'enjoyment' and gives her symbolic permission. The problem with women is that they are expected to submit to men as representing this place of God. But ah, men are not gods. And those readers who are men may have experienced how little women forgive you for that! Men are not all-Man either.

But still these disappointing effects do not prevent some women and men from carrying on the quest for this 'mystical' union, the quest for love. We have seen how this is attempted in some forms of eroticism where sexual enjoyment is achieved only if it is ecstatic, where one and/or the other of the partners lends themselves to represent God. This is the paradigm of the woman who has renounced *being him* in order to *have him* and then to *enjoy him*, precisely like a mystic. But only 'like' because, if women have access to that position, they are not all-mystic; they are in this position but they are not it. Other women cannot accept either this compromise between sex and divine ecstasy, or the one between man and God, and, of course, like Dora, they enjoy neither. Dora worships the Virgin, like Joseph, but misses God because, like a man, she has mistaken herself for him.

Dora wanted back her absolute and lost femininity, not her earthly sexual difference. Freud interpreted it as complicity and revenge against the father, almost as an act of accusation, rather than being able to listen to the dialectic of a woman's compliance and disagreement with her position. But Freud does not see femininity as a position but as a biological destiny. To Freud's question, 'What does a woman want', Dora's case answers: to be the Woman who does not exist. But to her question, 'What is a woman?', her case replies: the precious 'nothing' kept in the jewel case, the nothing which Mrs K. was for (or gave to) her husband. But, like her father, Freud does not know what a woman is. Although he would have liked to know, if only she had given him a chance; if only she had not fired him and had given him the satisfaction of curing her.

Both Freud and Dora were gambling with the downturned card of femininity which neither knew. They were both bluffing, and both were defeated. Freud challenged her femininity and she challenged the knowledge of the symbolic order in which Freud, father, Mr K. and herself expected her to be. And they were right, as Dora was in it, the way all humans, men and women, are. But she revealed the paradoxes that this order implied for her: paradoxes and conflicts which we might easily interpret and use as a paradigm to understand the ambivalent status of women in the symbolic order.

But in so far as Dora's silence, suicidal threats, slapping of Mr K. and the firing of Freud meant revenge and challenge, we are fully in the territory of human language, but with one who does not speak; like the woman described by Simone de Beauvoir, the woman who refuses to speak . . . what? The language of her own masters, that same language which should make her whole, give her an identity, and which has reduced her to no more than an object of a purely differential value and then of exchange between father and Mr K. In the hysterical woman the gap between language and our being comes to the fore, but as a discourse, still, as language then. Dora's illness functioned as an act of accusation against the father's law because the hysterical woman feels betrayed by it. When her father used Dora as an object of desire (for Mr K.), that is, by treating her as a woman, he unmasked her masculine identification. The idea that her father could satisfy Mrs K., that he was not impotent, and Mrs K. not self-sufficient like the Sistine Madonna she admired in Dresden, shattered Dora's hysterical scenario and her compliance with her father's affair. The virile seduction by Mr K. also shatters the hysterical dream of undesiring self-contentment.

Dora's unconscious response was then to put in question that law which gave her a soul in the first place but only to deprive her of it in the social exchange. But, by not consciously being able to admit this, her body paid for it. Her body became the battlefield where both the law (super-egoic law) and herself craved for revenge. This fragment of an analysis resembles in fact the fragment of a battle: Dora's hysterical rigour against Freud's rigorous law of the difference between the sexes. In the face of that law Dora vindicates her position like this: if the woman is nothing for you but an object-value, you will never be able to use or possess this no-object, like mother. If I am thus nothing, I will show you what this nothing 'is'; this nothing can slap you in the face; my body shall speak for me.

Various forms of feminism are further declensions of this feminine paradigm, still retaining to a higher or lesser degree the hysterical vindication and idealization of the woman's nothingness. Like Dora, feminists find it impossible to forgive the fact of being reduced to a sexed object of desire. Feminism is an attempt to decline the hysterical refusal to speak. The aggressivity and victimization that some forms of feminism take bear witness to its hysterical origins; that is, to a failure of articulation.

But if Dora was not a mystic, she was not a feminist either. There was no political stand; her strike was a solitary, unconscious one. She was not like her brother Otto Breuer, a famous revolutionary who helped to articulate the demands of the oppressed in Germany by organizing their strikes. Dora was engaged in this imaginary coincidence of nothingness and wholeness to the point of refusing any other desire, and her body suffered from refused desire. And she could not even take it when Freud tried (clumsily) to offer her a desire for Mr K.: instead, she felt nauseated. Desire was then replaced by . . . a discourse of love, with Freud complicit. Freud was caught up, too, in this confusion between love and desire. Dora did not in fact deny love for Mr K. or her father; she denied she desired them. But as desire cannot be annihilated, Dora desired . . . nothing, or rather desired an unfulfilled desire. She loved instead; she loved symbols, beauty, photos, presents and, most of all, the Virgin: the symbol of her androgyny, as the mother who conceived by herself without a penis.

By wanting to name the supposed objects of her desire, Freud lied for Dora because those objects were the refused objects of her desire. Dora assumed Freud to be lying to her and betraying her like her father, and when the analyst is suspected of lying there is no transference love: transference is love of the truth. But Dora herself was marked by the sign of deceit: her rebellion against father's deceit nevertheless aimed at veiling her own; she had become an accomplice of her father's affair with Mrs K. while having her own love affair with the latter. They both compete for the same woman and, at the same time, offer her to their rival.

The mark of deceit removes one farther and farther from truth; it reproduces itself. In spite of his counter-transference (or thanks to it) Freud was correct in pointing out a series of betrayals. If father betrayed her in a symbolic exchange, Dora betrayed father by revealing his affair, of which she was an accomplice, and by competing with him for the other woman. But Dora did not want to know anything about her own betrayals.

It was only after he had digested Dora's case that Freud became fully aware with another patient, a homosexual girl, of this '*Je n'en veux rien savoir*' ('I do not want to know anything about it'). The girl went to see Freud only to obey her father's desire to get rid of her homosexuality. Freud wrote: 'Once when I expounded to her a specially important part of the theory, one touching her, she replied in an inimitable tone "How very interesting", as though she were a *grande dame* being taken over a museum and glancing through her lorgnon at objects to which she was completely indifferent' (Freud 1920b, p. 163). This example is good because this patient had blatantly not chosen Freud's truth, she was *not* prepared to give up her homosexuality. In this case Freud seemed to recognize and respect her object choice: it is in that paper that he emphasized the original bisexuality in human beings.

It is obvious in this case that Freud is very sceptical about the girl's treatment; in fact, this time, unlike with Dora, he broke it off. He advised her to continue only with a woman therapist, and then only if her parents really 'set store by the therapeutic procedure' (ibid.).

Probably Freud was led to refuse her treatment because her indifference reminded him of Dora's. But was it the same kind of indifference, the same, 'I don't want to know anything about it'? I do not think so. Whereas this girl had accepted her status of homosexual, and the ensuing conflicts with her father, Dora had kept her indifference disguised and fooled Freud up to the end, when her departure took him by surprise; she fired him with indifference. This is the hysterical ambiguity. The homosexual patient, instead, openly desired her beloved lady, and thereupon, under external pressure she could give her up in the end, but only to retain her homosexuality; that is, she could contemplate giving up one object but retained her own desire for other possible objects.

But when men demanded Dora as an object of desire or offered themselves as objects, her love and her desire to be loved presented themselves as pure resistance. She was looking for a purity of love in repudiating its objects. That is why she could not even admit her hatred towards them, her craving for revenge, as Freud called it. Hysteria in this case appears like a failure to vindicate the role of the other, or a wish to disagree with the law of the phallic signifier for being subjected to it. But what holds the hysteric from revealing her disagreement is her basic complicity with the phallic law. She cannot give up an identification which ties her to it; maybe compliance and disagreement are the signs at a crossroads which every woman has to go over because of her paradoxical position in the symbolic order. The homosexual patient, for example, chose to slip away from the symbolic order represented by her father, although this implied that she was being overwhelmed when placed in front of her father's angry gaze. In opposition to most male homosexuals, who enjoy women's company, lesbians usually evade the presence of men because they have evaded their order. When Freud's young homosexual was caught in the street by her father's eyes she wanted only to disappear, attempting suicide, as if lesbians prefer to die when placed in front of the trapping eyes of the law of sexual difference. Dora did not want to die; she was ill. Her illness let the law of the symbolic order thrust into her flesh and be retained on her body like a hair shirt.

Part III

7

A Myth in Development: The Case of Little Hans

A little boy of four and a half, from a well-educated family, whose parents had embraced new psychoanalytical ideas about how to bring up a child, became phobic.

> His parents were both among my closest adherents, and they had agreed that in bringing up their first child they would use no more coercion than might be absolutely necessary for maintaining good behaviour. And as the child developed into a cheerful, good-natured and lively little boy, the experiment of letting him grow up and express himself without being intimidated went on satisfactorily. (Freud, 1909, p. 6)

But at the fatal age of four, the experimentally bred, cheerful, lively little boy started to show signs of disturbance. Libertarian upbringing had worked well throughout the pre-Oedipal age, but something was not working exactly at the age which Freud himself called Oedipal. Why? According to Freud the pedagogic experiment was not carried as far as venturing to give Hans 'the last piece of enlightenment', about the existence of the vagina and of copulation. But, in a later passage, Freud considers the limits the power of upbringing has upon predispositions to neurotic diseases. Freud seemed slightly disturbed at witnessing an uninhibited upbringing stop working at that turning point he himself had discovered.

Could we then do away with the problem, being more Freudian than Freud, just by saying the Freudian Oedipus complex, this turning point in everybody's psychic development, is in itself a point of inevitable crisis and disturbance, before which no educational intervention holds total power? In a certain sense it is true, but not a satisfactory answer, in so far as not all four-year-old children are pathologically phobic at that point and not all of them, thank God, have to turn to a psychoanalyst because of the Oedipus complex. What is the Oedipus complex, then, and the peculiarity which makes it an unavoidable milestone of the human unconscious?

With Dora we looked at the unconscious conflicts which erupted in her hysterical symptoms. In Dora we could detect a pre-Oedipal stage, where the subject's main relationship is generally with the mother, whose traces we detected in her secret, the mystery of her knowledge about her mother's body, as well as her own body and other women's in general. But Dora's further development seemed to be cut from this original experience, which appeared removed in the mystery of her symptoms. The rest of her psychic development was structured around the paternal figure, who took over in spite of the ensuing conflicts. So, in Dora, too, we witness retroactively something which was not resolved at this point of passage. The Oedipus installed an unconscious conflict in Dora which was never solved: a withdrawing of the maternal figure, a lacking figure which she was homosexually to look for in other women; and the paternal intervention as a saviour in her first dream.

If in Dora's case her feminine Oedipus is determined by the lack of the maternal figure, we might be led to the hypothesis that the paternal figure might have played a similar lacking role in the masculine Oedipus in little Hans. Freud's conviction was that the father had not fulfilled all the requirements of the therapy, as his discourse stopped short of the vagina and coitus. But could Hans's father's shortcomings as a therapist not hide the fact that he did not fulfil something else in relation to his son? We might suspect that the father needed the application of psychoanalysis and the intervention of Freud himself in order to fill that gap. Let us read, with Lacan, Hans's production of dreams and phantasies as a description of his father's position in relation to Hans.

'Long before he was in the world, I had known that a little Hans would come who would be so fond of his mother that he would be bound to feel afraid of his father because of it.' (Freud, 1909, p. 42). This is the Oedipus myth as Freud formulated it for Hans; but we could now look at the way the boy responded to it, the way he developed it, as it were. If we assume a lack in the figure of the father, Hans's phobia should tell us something about it. It first manifested itself as agoraphobia and then as a horse phobia. But as the psychoanalytical treatment, conducted by his own father, went on, his phobic object went through a chain of transformations: the horses frightened him only when starting off, then only when loaded with a heavy cart, and then there was a fear of missing trains, and so on, like an infinite chain of deferments and movements. All of Hans's phobia seems to be, in fact, a description of a passage, and of missing it; it is like the enacting of the drama of movement away from something towards something else. And the means of transport became the phobic objects: horses, carts, trains; barriers to infringe and overcome. So, in this setting off, from one place to another, or from one means of transport to another, anxiety arises. Freud looked at it only in terms of the unwillingness of the child to lose his close relationship with mother; we would like to look at it from the perspective of the movement away from mother; a double anxiety.

We all may have experienced, even beyond our fourth year of life, an occasion when at a railway station we have said our goodbyes to someone very dear to us, and at the same time we have to run to catch the train which is starting off and which is not going to wait for us. We are going to take our destined train, no matter if by reason of our own will, of pleasure, of necessity, or of duty. But we are doing it only at the cost of losing something, separating from what had appeared so far our only reality and destiny. But if Oedipus is only a myth and neither an instinct, a physiological necessity nor a developmental stage, why then have we all to go through it? Exactly because it reflects the law of separation raised to a psychic phenomenon, it is the painful rite of separation which initiates the law of castration. Until then the child has no pressing need to elaborate psychically his/her sense of separation from mother, the trauma of birth, or of her devouring desires; the child can still enact and recuperate them within the dual relationship with the mother. S/he is not required to leave the mother; on the contrary, what is required of him/her is to feel at one with the mother's body in order to fill and satisfy the mother's desire to be One, to have her human and feminine void filled by a child. In that sense one can say that the child accomplishes the function of the mother's phallus for a certain time, and in some cases for all his/her life.

For the moment we can say that, in general, for the first few years of a child's life, his/her vision of the world does not need to go beyond the mother's relatively small circuit, as Lacan called it, which even if not lacking in conflicts and traumas, still offers a psychic illusion of bodily satisfaction and a sense of unity. The baby is allowed an imaginary clinging on to a lost real unity with the mother's body, to the vestiges of an original experience which can only slowly be given up by both partners involved.

And what about the father at this stage? Psychoanalysts from various schools have given different emphasis to the paternal function in the pre-Oedipal age, but for all of them the father seems to appear as a figure that is mediated. For Melanie Klein, for example, the father is contained in the mother's body as an imaginary penis and the child fights his/her battles with it within the maternal circuit, which was for Klein the inside of the mother's body. This penis is one of the mother's attributes and possessions the child has to live with, usually in great conflict.

On the contrary, for Lacan, the father plays a part in relation to what is lacking in the mother, and to what she desires in spite of her child. So, also in Lacan, the father represents a problematic figure, the obstacle to the idyllic symbiotic relationship with mother. The father represents the limits of that wholeness and unmasks the illusion. The father is placed at the threshold between a mythical originary experience with mother's body and the human development into the human law, with all its social and cultural rules and roles. But the father represents also an opening towards something else, a bigger circuit, with other possibilities, maybe illusory too, but like a new, more advanced game for older children, where one has to read the instructions first if one wants to play and enjoy it. The rules of the game – those are what is represented symbolically by the father.

This symbolic father marks the existence of another enjoyment than the 'real' one, but only in demanding the abandonment of the previous one. Freud compared the symbolic father to the figure of God, an entity who lives in higher and larger spheres, the enjoyable heaven, where we are all destined to go one day; but meanwhile we usually wish to enjoy our mother earth and we fear death, which going to God would entail. Yes, we complain about the pain of living, how unbearable, senseless, disappointing life is, but we basically fear death. Maybe this is the Oedipal conflict hovering between mother's earth and father's ethereal spheres; it must be like facing death. The 'panic' of the Roman initiate (plate 4) witnesses that such an encounter took place in those rites, as well as in psychoanalysis. The result of this encounter, of going through it and surviving it, is what Lacan calls symbolic castration. Castration is then the representative of death in our life, but it is not it. We will see how in little Hans, as for the neurotic in general, this representative is taken for the thing in itself. Neurotics try desperately to evade castration as if their own life were at stake. For little Hans the possession of a penis was the sign of being alive; inanimate things do not have a 'widdler'. Hans's reaction to the Oedipal stage was a reaction to the introduction of the signifier of death in his life, although the signifier is, paradoxically, meant to enrich and develop it. This does not mean that the real father has necessarily to accomplish this deadly function, but he certainly represents it, like Hans's father.

We might wonder at this point why, whether with or without a father, the child finds himself at this threshold at that particular point. Why is he expected to be there, then; why can the old game not be sustained any more? In order to answer these questions let us look at Hans and what is happening to his life at that point. His language was starting to structure itself around some basic concepts – widdler = animate, no widdler = inanimate – which were not adequate and which his parents would have been expected to clarify for him, as they had done until then. He could not believe the stork story or that mother had a widdler as all evidence was against it. But at that point Hans, who was trotting forward like a horse, as one would expect of a child who had been brought up in a progressive and enlightened way, found his parents behind, probably for the first time. If a liberal upbringing had been easier to offer to a toddler, it did not seem to be that easy any more as the child was growing older. The parents' enlightened views stumbled over masturbation, copulation, birth and sexual difference. Hans's parents could not reveal to their baby the secrets of a more adult life, however much they consciously wanted to do so and however much it would have been consistent to expect it from them.

It is in the father's reports to Freud that we can get a glimpse of some double-bind interaction between Hans and his parents. While, on the one hand, the mother was threatening him with castration in relation to his masturbation, rejecting as piggish his attempts at seducing her, on the other hand she put on a jealousy scene when

Hans showed his determination to go to bed with another girl; the mother rejected his penis, symbol so far of all living enjoyment and desires for Hans, but she kept him in bed with her in spite of her husband's protests (to his wife, not to Hans). The father looks like the loser in relation to Hans, while the mother seems to be in charge of the child's movements and trajectories. The father was there like an effigy of a father; he represented, in a tantalizing way, the world of separation from mother and of masculinity for Hans, but he was not able to intervene to give him a real and willing hand – not until Hans himself, with his phobia, warned him. About what? That father was missing the train in which he should have taken his son with him away from mother. And father became a therapist, he hurried up to catch the train of psychoanalysis; the real father took up the symbolic function thanks to Freud's intervention. Father was trotting after the son trying to digest Freud's myth of Oedipus, which he had obviously not digested himself. Freud offered it to Hans as an instrument of cure, a key, which the boy was looking for to record and overhaul his world. And with Hans we can also overhaul the Oedipus myth, and its effects.

Hans's anxiety does not seem to have arisen as an effect of the Oedipus complex as such, but on the contrary, because of a difficulty, a barrier he found in its development. We have the two sides of his anxiety again: one related to his desire to leave the place which had become too small for him, and the other of not being able to start off all by himself. But one might wonder why did he want to start off: who was demanding that he should leave his mother? Even though, in an ambiguous way, his mother was. And her ambiguity leads one to ask: what did the mother want from her child? 'What do you want?': this is the question which inaugurates the Oedipus, a questioning which the oracle can never answer adequately. And when the oracle did answer Oedipus, who questioned it on his destiny, he misinterpreted it. In order to run away from his destiny he ran into it. The real and symbolic parents represented by the two parental sets, Polybus and his wife, and Laius and Jocasta, were all involved in the covering of Oedipus' destiny; they cannot tell him the truth if not ambiguously, inadequately.

So, the mother too cannot admit she is not One with her child, she desires something else, or more. Hans was learning what his mother did not want; she did not want his penis or that he should give it to other girls, and ultimately she gave birth to another child who came to fill the place Hans had enjoyed before, and a child with such a small widdler too! Alas, lost Garden of Eden! The penis as a symbol of enjoyment and life can be actually cut off or not be there, and the mother threatened him with castration. I would not be surprised if Hans desired to run away from mother's arbitrary laws of rejection and seduction. This is the moment in which the father usually intervenes in order to encourage the separation from the mother. Only through entering a masculine world with his father could he save his penis, but only by hiding it away with decency. Remember the stage when Hans wished that his father made him 'widdle' away from the look of other children, in opposition to his previous exhibitionism. This is symbolic castration, and its compensation will be the phallus. Here it is what mother had wanted, what was lacking to both of them. The phallus is not an object or a phantasy, but the symbol of an object that is not there. It is what in antiquity was called a *simulacrum*, the image and the representation of a god to be worshipped. For Lacan the phallus is the symbol of the object *par excellence*, the symbol of reference for all the other symbols. It stands for what is beyond the opening of the mother's body, as what should ideally fulfil her desire which not even children can fulfil.

But Hans's father was at pains to take up the function of the symbolic father. His position appears ambiguous too, in relation to the phallus; he seems to leave Hans without a replacement for the threatened penis. Although he was lurking at the threshold of the big circuit, he could not take the horse role and ride away with his son. The horse is in fact Hans's phobic object. Why, if no horse is going to ride away with him? But anxiety arises exactly because of this confrontation of the subject with an absence, a want of being in which he is captured and lost. Anxiety does not seem to have an object. And it is in front of this anxiety that the subject constructs the phobic object, a replacement for nothingness which is represented by the mother's lack of a penis.

The horse concentrated in itself all the contradictions and ambiguities of Hans's position. A horse is big, strong and beautiful, has got a big widdler and is a symbol of independence; it runs away wherever it likes. This was the image of the adult world for Hans. In fact, the father and especially the mother were compared to a horse before the phobia started; he wondered if mother had a widdler like a horse. No distinction between the sexes seemed to play any part in Hans's mind at this stage. In this pre-Oedipal stage the widdler played the role of the phallus, but *an imaginary one*, we could say a pre-Oedipal one. It was not as yet the signifier of sexual separation and difference: feminine and masculine worlds were equivalent for Hans. The widdler functioned already as a symbol, but a symbol of the power of all living things; it was placed imaginarily on the mother's body and it dictated from there. That was the stage when Hans was living in an objectively symbiotic relationship with his mother, until his first summer holiday at three and a half. Until then he enjoyed almost exclusively the company of his mother and did not see other children: a boy raised in the city life style, which is the largest breeding ground of modern neurosis.

The change in his life was triggered off by his new experiences outside his mother's space; when on his summer holiday he came into contact with children and new people, he tasted new flavours, new pleasures and excitements, he met girls and boys to fall in love with – he was in a bigger space. And, of course, once we come to experience and know something new, there is no going back to the old ignorance; we lose our innocence, as it were. Then, back in Vienna, the world was not the same any more for Hans. The shock seemed to have been such that he crossed any reference to the holiday experience out of his mind, only to make it become the core of his phantasies later on, after another extraordinary event: the birth of a sister.

Undoubtedly, the mother's dual little world was not the same any more; an external world seemed to have entered Hans's room. The horse, the beautiful animal which rides outside, entered Hans's room; his phobia started with this perturbing phantasy. Another image, then, came to my mind from one of my childhood books, *Alice in Wonderland*: a picture of Alice when she had grown so much that her legs, arms and head stuck out of the house's doors and windows, trapped in her own place. In the same way Hans's phobia seems to represent both the outside breaking into the familiar inside and claustro-agoraphobia at being stuck inside. The phobia seems also to reproduce the new, shattering realization of sexual difference at his sister's birth.

But the emergence of this realization cannot be without consequences for the child's pre-Oedipal phallus, namely, the mother's phallus. What becomes of it? Some of my analysands' phantasies which characterize this stage gave me the idea of a metamorphic representation of the all-powerful maternal imaginary phallus, which undergoes a sort of perforation in the child's mind; it must bear a difference. An analysand with obsessive symptoms would describe his horror of snakes which can throw poison at you from inside their mouths, which he associated with the sight of pubic hair. The sight of it made him transfixed and impotent, as if he were immobilized in a gaze. He had confessed that he had never learned that women had no penis until he was an adolescent. Even then he rejected the idea. He associated this female penis with something threatening: a crocodile's jaws. Like the asexual horse which had become for Hans a biting horse, a dangerous opening which could bite his finger, in the same way the crocodile could devour my analysand inside its body.

The Italian fairy tale 'Pinocchio' is a very effective description of the devouring phantasy many children have. Pinocchio is swallowed by a whale and his father comes to save him from the inside of the whale. The maternal penis becomes hollow and the animal takes on the sexual mark of a vagina, but a phallic one. For one analysand the maternal phallus had become a giant hollow tube awaiting its prey: once, when he was playing as a child inside such a tube, he felt like fainting.

Certainly, as Freud said, what had once been enjoyable, in the main, later becomes anguishing through the work of repression. Certainly; but one can wonder why Hans needed to repress it, if his father had not threatened him about his desire to be inside mother. Because, as the examples have just shown, it was a maternal space which had become threatening and rejecting in the child's imaginary, as if the illusion of enjoying the 'real' of mother's body were unavoidably shattered.

When the father asked Hans whom he would like to beat, mummy, sister or him, he promptly answered 'Mummy'. This sadistic wish, and it was no accident that it was drawn out by his father, leads me to think that sadism might arise in connection with this shattered image of the lost object, which is, then, to be destroyed, forgotten, repressed in order for us to go on and trot away.

So, the frightening horse is the shattered image of the maternal phallus: the horse is at first beautiful and powerful, but, wait a moment, the horse is also used. It is attached to a loaded cart, it is whipped and enslaved; there are, thus, different kinds, or better, say, *genders* of horses. And Hans feared those horses which represented this difference, the sexual difference. This gave him anxiety because the recognition of it would have made him recognize mother's castration. In fact, not only had she not got a widdler, but she was not supposed to have the phallus either. The denigration women have always suffered, if only from being called the weaker sex, this subordination of the feminine to the phallic order, is an infantile attempt to liberate oneself from the mother's original power.

Here we are, plunged into the master–slave dialectic, which the horse with all its contradictory aspects represented very well for Hans. But the horse also had a function of mediation, attachment and linkage between two worlds; it replaced a lack of linkage and of a phallus. We can see how the horse, a real object, let us say a signified, was elevated in Hans's phobia to the function of signifier, and it was as a signifier that it played a constitutive role, but not as a univocal symbol. Like all signifiers, it worked only with other signifiers. It signified both the movement itself from one place to another, from one signifier to another, and the blockage in the movement. No place can be left empty; all places are left to other signifiers: the movement became the cart which slowed it down, the cart became a train which was going to be missed, and so on in a chain of deferments.

Lacan (1956–7) pointed out three movements Hans feared most in the horse: (1) when *it started off*, that is, the anxiety about his own starting off and the movement which can drop him; (2) when *it bit* like the crocodile's jaws in the case above; (3) when *it fell*: the fall of a world . . . and the fall of birth too, the birth of his sister who had put Hans in front of his double, as what he himself was for his mother. The sister represented him as both an idealized and castrated phallus, the baby, the king.

The birth event unchained the signifier of the origins and their mystery, the mystery of separation. It was signified by the horse which had become a loaded cart, a pregnant tummy which dropped its 'lumfs' as well as its phallus. In this way castration and delivery were connected in one signifier. The unconscious complex of castration has the function of a knot in the human assumption of sexual identity. Freud thought that humans could assume sexual identity only through threat of a privation, and that it constituted an essential disturbance in human sexuality. In fact the object of desire as real seems to be lost for us. We are left with its representatives, or, like Hans, with a phobic object which masks anxiety because of the lack of it; the horse was a screen object. The 'real' is always at the limits of the analytical experience and psychoanalysis deals with the holes of the 'real', namely, with language. It constitutes a world of symbolic objects, a world where humanity abides and where it can create an order in which the holes can be given a meaning and tolerated. Myths are the allegorical figures on which symbolic rites are based. Freud goes back to the mysteric symbol of the phallus which was already then the symbol of symbolism itself, because it never got unveiled; it gets confused with the veil itself.

This difference was anguishing for Hans because it effected a split in him to which he could not easily find a solution. He was lost in the world of symbols; he was looking for points of reference, indeed for myths. Hans needed a myth, and Freud gave him one. Consider Hans's dream of the two giraffes, one real and the other crumpled like paper. Yes, he could take possession of the crumpled one (the mother) thanks to his widdler, as Freud interpreted the dream. But all he could take possession of was a piece of crumpled paper, while the phallus was crying out his rights. If the real giraffe was the father as the upholder of the symbolic world and of the phallus, it had certainly become more real than his previous babyish state with the mother.

A decisive step towards Hans's cure was achieved when the father told him that women had no penises. Hans reacted with a hyper-production of phantasies whose function was to restructure his imaginary and symbolic world. His phantasies displayed, one after the other, all the possible and impossible solutions or developments he could give to the myth, so nicely put to him by Freud. And we could take our turn after Freud and Hans for developing and reformulating a myth: a little boy was born whose widdler has been denied by the mother, but thanks to his father he can, willy-nilly, take leave of maternal omnipotence and be given symbolic virility, but not a real virility, not yet.

But Hans expressed it better in the last of a long series of phantasies: 'the plumber came and took away his behind with a pair of pincers, and then gave him another, and then did the same with his widdler.' This is the phantasy which should synthesize the solution or non-solution Hans gave to his Oedipus. A man from outside comes in, not a horse or father, but rather a *deus ex machina*. This is what Freud was for him: his plumber. This man is not running after him, but, as a matter of fact, takes his old behind, an earlier erogenous part, to give him another one; Hans does not say bigger, but it was certainly another one, not the original one, but a constructed, artificial one. And the same for his widdler: an ambiguous formulation which makes it doubtful whether Hans was still trying to spare his penis from all this. But certainly Hans could not spare his behind from this transformation, this dramatic exchange, so peculiar to the human kind, the one between a mythical original state and the equally mythical state of culture.

8

Winnicott's 'Piggle'

After little Hans, the Freudian child, we pass now to discussing another clinical case from the child-analysis literature, D.W. Winnicott's 'Piggle' (Winnicott, 1989). I have already mentioned this case in chapter 3. Here, I will discuss it in more depth. The Piggle is a little girl of two years old who is affected by a phobic symptomatology.

Little Hans's phobia described well the Freudian understanding of phobia, in 'Inhibitions, symptoms and anxiety' (Freud, 1926) as a particular form of anxiety. Unlike obsessional neurosis in adults, where anxiety does not seem to have a specific object, the phobic child or adult elects an object as cause of anxiety in the form of fear. Little Hans feared horses, but not any horse. He feared those who got stuck, who fell or stopped. Hans's phobic object was a stuck, fixed object. The horse started to move and change into other objects (trains, carriages, a plumber, etc.) only as an effect of the analytical work. The neurotic instead displaces its objects of anxiety most of the time. They function like the infectious taboos of the obsessionals (Freud, 1913). We would say that in an adult's anxiety, the object is disguised by being displaced. In a phobia instead, *anxiety is not without an object* as it gets caught and fixed in an object around which the world of the child is frozen. Nothing moves; the beautiful and powerful horse stops and falls. The fall of a world!

Child neurosis announces itself with phobic symptoms half-way between adult neurosis and perversion.[1] If early childhood functions under pre-genital eroticism, an eroticism where sexual difference does not play a key role in one's own sexual identity, little Hans's polymorphous perversion indicated his pre-Oedipal libidinal economy, in which the perverse structure finds its satisfaction. This passage from the polymorphous perversion of infancy into the Oedipal drama of sexual differentiation finds its compromise in phobia.

The Piggle also presented herself with a more or less fixed phobia, but unlike Hans's external horse, her objects are her own inner creation. They appear only out of darkness, a night phobia in the place of dreams, or, more accurately, by not letting her sleep, these objects come to interrupt her dreams. She has two recurrent 'awake' nightmares: black mummy and babacar. What are they, hallucinations, dreams, phantasies? I mentioned that for Freud anxiety, unlike phobia, lacks an object. It signals an unknown danger. It is unknown because it is an 'instinctual danger' coming from the subject itself. Piggle fears the blackness of the dark and of seeing something where nothing should be seen. In this loss of light, in this absence of visible objects, the black object appears, black like death.

The death drive is conspicuously absent in Winnicott's theoretical framework, even though in this case it breaks into the sessions in the form of the train which the Piggle takes every time she comes to see him in London from Oxford on her own demand. Once in the session her main activities are pulling, linking and playing with trains, carriages, planes, engines. Like Hans she has a mobile signifier, the 'babacar' (baby car?), which is stuck in the black and which carries blackness. She goes to Winnicott because she is told that Dr Winnicott knows about babacars and black mummies, and she wants to know about them. Later she will tell her mother: 'Dr Winnicott does not know about babacars.' But when towards the end of her analysis she asked her mother to see Winnicott again to tell him all about babacars, and her mother comments that she must already know all about them then, Piggle replies: 'I don't know but I can tell him.'

She had learned by now not only that Winnicott is not supposed to know all about babacars, and nor is she, but that in telling him, she will find speech says more than we know. Hans too knew that the 'nonsense' was his own, although Freud, like Winnicott, had to help to get rid of it by listening to what he had to say through his production of phantasies and dialogues with his father. The Piggle tells Winnicott by playing instead. Whereas Freud followed the development of Hans's production of phantasies, Winnicott follows the development of her play and her 'enjoyment'[2] in it. For Winnicott, enjoying the game means allowing the unconscious to communicate. Like Freud he thinks that the child's playing is a way of mastering anxiety concerned with the dialectic presence/absence. Anxiety has to do with absence, or rather with an object as being absent, the way a ghost stands for the dead person. So Winnicott listens to these night ghosts which come out of her play and her words, and while enacting them himself he engages her in a dialogue, acted or spoken, where, in Winnicott's words, 'the nascent unconscious' is verbalized in the terms of transference.

Another point in common between Hans and the Piggle is the relation of their parents to the analyst. The Piggle's (or Gabrielle's) parents are Winnicottian as much as Hans's parents were Freudian (Hans's mother had been Freud's analysand and Gabrielle's mother's letters show a harmonious agreement with Winnicott's therapy). It is mainly through the mother's words and her letters to Winnicott that Piggle's case proceeds and is presented to us. We have a hint here as to what Lacan meant when he said that the child is the symptom of his/her parents. Gabrielle's mother hints continuously at her own anxiety (her jealousy when she had a sib at the same age as Gabrielle, her guilt at having had a second baby too soon), as if her expectations and desires were part and parcel of Piggle's night anxiety attacks.

The introductory description of the Piggle is made by her mother (just as Hans's was made by his father). She writes that as a baby Gabrielle was

> very much a person with great inner resources . . . Her balance had been excellent always, but since the change in her she had been falling and crying and feeling hurt. She used to be high-handed. Her mother was simply someone to be ordered around. From the age of six months, she adored her father, and at that age said: 'Daddy!' But she soon forgot or ceased to be able to use the word. Since the change, she seemed to see mother as a separate person, and had become affectionate with her, and at the same time more reserved toward her father . . . We never told you about her as a baby; she seemed remarkably composed and sure of touch, giving one the feeling that she had authority within her world. We tried hard, and I think successfully, to protect her from impingements which would make her world too complicated. When Susan was born, Gabrielle seemed somehow thrown out of her mold, and cut off from her sources of nourishment.

We found it hurtful to see her so diminished and reduced, and she
may well have sensed this. There was also a period of tension between us two [the parents]. (Winnicott, 1989, pp. 14, 20)

Three themes come to the fore: (1) an overprotective upbringing,
which Winnicott will criticize in a subtle way in one of his letters to
the parents; (2) the very early attachment to her father (six months
of age, with a detachment from her mother), and her self-contained
bearing as a baby; (3) the catastrophic change after her sister's birth,
which changes her from an overconfident baby into a 'shy' little girl
(as she introduces herself to Winnicott on her very first visit).

She presents herself in almost the opposite terms to those her
mother had used to describe her as a baby: she is a frightened little
thing, and mostly, all her preoccupations are around mummy; a
black one, but still a mummy! And she has a declared 'shyness' ('I
am too shy') towards Winnicott that contradicts her previous closeness to her father, a shyness she will not keep very long, and her
father will soon be taking a big part in Piggle's sessions at a real
level. But it is remarkable how Winnicott plays down Piggle's relation to her father at a psychoanalytical level. This goes hand in hand
with his being oblivious of his interpretations about sexual intercourse provoking anxiety, being felt by Piggle as an attempt at
seduction.

When she replies, 'I've got a cat, next time I'll bring the pussycat,
another day', she is not only temporizing before opening the door to
find protection with her mother: she is also answering his sexual
'provocation'. We could say that Winnicott is completely oblivious
to the idea of an excess of closeness in the father–daughter relation,
as well as of his own physical and psychic excess of closeness to
Gabrielle. According to object-relations theories, Oedipal conflicts
are present in the infant very early on, and that is perhaps why a
remarkable early object-choice for the father did not seem to surprise Winnicott. But I was struck by the fact that this attachment
appeared to be an early, pre-Oedipal choice, whereas Klein talks
about pre-Oedipal conflicts where the father appears as an obstacle
to the total enjoyment of the mother. But, as with little Hans, it is a
baby sister who unchains the Oedipal drama, a drama for at least
three people. The baby arrives and divides; the baby enters as a
third term which overturns Gabrielle's dual vision of the world. The

birth of Hanna had intervened to break Hans's symbiotic relation with his mother, but he could not find in his real father the support for this separation. His father, like Gabrielle's parents, could not say no.

The birth of Piggle's sister finds her pre-Oedipally attached to her father, the way Hans was to his mother. Piggle has elected her father as her own generator. So in order to find a position which will allow her to go through the Oedipal drama as it is set in the myth, she has to recover or reclaim the mother back, as we'll see in the second session, which I quote below.

Me: 'Winnicott very greedy baby; want all the toys.'

She kept asking for just one toy, but I repeated what I was required to say in this game. Eventually she took one toy out to her father in the waiting room. I thought I heard her say: 'Baby want all the toys.' After a while she brought this toy back and she seemed very pleased that I was being greedy.

Piggle: 'Now the Winnicott baby has all the toys. I'll go to Daddy.'

Me: 'You are afraid of the greedy Winnicott baby, the baby that was born out of the Piggle and that loves the Piggle and that wants to eat her.'

She went to her father and tried to shut the door as she left. I heard the father working overtime in the waiting room trying to entertain her, because (of course) *he did not know where he was in this game.*

I told the father to come into the room now, and the Piggle came in with him. She got on his lap and said: 'I am shy.'

After a while she showed her father the Winnicott baby, this monster she had given birth to . . . While performing acrobatics on her father's lap she told him all the details. Then she started a new and very deliberate chapter in the game. 'I'm a baby too,' she announced, *as she came out head first onto the floor between her father's legs.*

Me: 'I want to be the only baby. I want all the toys.'

Piggle: 'You've got all the toys.'

Me: 'Yes, but I want to be the only baby; I don't want there to be any more babies.'

[She got on her father's lap again and was born again.]

Piggle: 'I'm the baby too.'

She went on being born from father's lap onto the floor . . . 'I'm just born. And it wasn't black inside.'

She had now developed a technique for being the baby while allowing me to represent herself.

There came a new development. She was now having a different way of being born out of the top of the father's head. (Winnicott, 1989, pp. 27, 30: my italics)

Take note that after being born from the father she says, 'I am just born, and it wasn't black inside', to reply to Winnicott's interpretation. She denies she was ever born from black insides; she was born from the bright areas of father's mind. But the babacar, the baby, like a car, brings the mother back to the subject, who rediscovers the mother as a lost object. But this return of the mother costs Piggle her identity. She in fact never answered as herself but as if she were the little sister Susan; her return to mother is attempted through an identification with her sister.

She says: 'Babacar moves blackness from one place to another.' It is like the undesired return of the repressed, which spreads itself around, and against which we can only erect a symptom such as a phobic object or an 'awake' nightmare.

The first half of her analysis unfolds within this vicious circle: the denied mother returns under the form of this black mummy who wants her yams (= breasts), and here Winnicott does not spare Piggle the interpretations of a greedy and cannibalistic baby. But Winnicott will enact the baby, treating the babacar both as the means of transport towards the mother and as what makes mummy black. The mother emerges out of darkness; she is made visible in relation to the other baby. Winnicott will have to inject (in a Kleinian way, as we will see in the next chapter) a sibling jealousy whereas Piggle could only identify with her sister in an attempt to recuperate her own mother–baby relation.

To this indirect encounter with the black mummy, Piggle responds with anxiety, and it is at this point that she brings her father into the session. Her father is brought in as if he had to protect her from the dangerous baby-Winnicott, the jealous baby. She has to bring the real father in because Winnicott is coming closer to a mother whom only a father, a third person, can placate.

There is then an overturning of positions: once the father has been introduced into the analytical session, the work can carry on

(Winnicott: 'she needs her father to communicate to me'). There are three of them now: the function of the father has been introduced through the real father, who does not know where he is in the game, though. It will soon be shown in the session how the real father is introduced as the third to protect Piggle from the voracious monster-Winnicott which she herself has created. But once introduced, the father takes his original place as the 'maternal father' (the generator), and Winnicott is placed in the position of the third, their witness. The place of the father, at this point, is interchangeable.

It is only by establishing this dynamic triangle that Piggle can describe her own fundamental phantasy: she reproduces the scene of her birth from her father's body down his legs repeatedly, and at last she reproduces her birth from his head. She is born from her father, from her father's head where it is not dark. Eric Laurent (1981) calls it the myth of Athena, born all armed from her father's head. The father functions here as a defence against the black mother; takes her place, as it were. The symbolic dimension of the myth sweeps away, but only momentarily, the imaginary fabrications of blackness, thus producing a temporary relief from black mummy. She gets better but the myth of Athena does not work for long: it is a symbolically precarious one based on flight from blackness. Her 'wee' needs a doctor: 'She looked very confused, and she said: "I am angry with my daddy." "Why?" "Because I love him too much"' (p. 32). Here we have the little analysand's own Oedipal interpretation. We see the unconscious working on the shift from one myth to the other, the acknowledgement of a 'too much'. And here we come to the third passage.

In this, the black mother, unsuccessfully repressed earlier in her flight to her father, returns like the return of the repressed. The Piggle relapses in her phobias; black mummy seizes her at night to claim her right to exist. She claims her back through the baby and tinges everything with her dark colour. A turning point from this circularity of anxiety and defence (her flight towards the father every time she is seized by anxiety with Winnicott) takes place in the ninth session when she reveals her dream about black mummy:

'I dreamed she was dead. She wasn't there.' At this point she did something which I am sure had great significance, whatever it symbolized. I could tell this from the fact that the whole quality of the session altered. It was as if everything else had been held back for this

to happen. She took the blue eyebath and put it in and out of her
mouth, making sucking noises, and it could be said that she experienced something very near to a generalized orgasm. (Winnicott, 1989,
pp. 117–18)

The object of maternal *jouissance*, or as Winnicott calls it, of generalized orgasm, is re-encountered as a partial object, detached from
mother. But this time she does not attach the object to father either;
she is left enjoying alone with this eyebath. And then Gabrielle says
the words: 'I loved her very much . . . who shot mummy?' Therefore
the acknowledgement of the dead mother leaves her with an object
of orgasm, an object which does not belong to either. It is an object
'too much', to be dropped.

Winnicott puts the accent on the positivity of this event; the two
split aspects of the mother, bad and good, come together – the
orgiastically eaten and shot, ambivalent mother. But I would put a
stress on its aspect as farewell, a farewell to a dead mother whom
she loved very much and to the *jouissance* that her death entailed for
her, her solitary masturbation. The oral link with mother is replaced
by a detachable object she can suck or replace with the father's penis
in her later phantasies. It seems therefore that in order not to lose
her mother she has to lose this object and the solitary enjoyment it
entails. The transitional object, this compromise between me/not
me, cannot hold. We can see the Oedipal conflict emerging here. It is
making one's own accounts with the parental other from which we
can only take flight at our own cost. The Piggle's is a funerary
enjoyment more than a transitional one.

After this turning point she is naked and disidentified. Her un-
successful identification with Susan gives way to an identification
with mother. She hides in her mother's dressing gowns. By putting
herself in mother's clothes she could get into the Other, give herself
back to mother as a part-object. This is a regression to a pre-Mirror
Stage, when one's own image as separate from mother is not yet
constituted. She is inside the maternal envelope. This regression
seems necessary for the Oedipal stage to set in analysis. The
eleventh session is all about snipping, cutting strings and pulling
trains; she asks Winnicott to use his scissors and thanks him when
he does so. It is the right cut which is in question now, to drop

herself from being her mother's object, the cutting loose of an object which binds us to a *jouissance* to be dropped.

She starts to let things out of herself; she stops tidying up obsessively all the toys in Winnicott's room before going, she leaves the mess behind as well as her smells (her overcoming of anal retention). So all the previous stages of anxiety lead in the last part of her analysis to castration anxiety and to her identification with father; but also, maybe, to an identification with the little boy that her mother was expecting instead of another daughter, or the little brother her mother was jealous of, or the little boy mother wanted to be. In any case her wee is sore and needs white cream. The object *a*, the lacking object, is here represented at the level of genitality, that is, of sexual difference. The wound is in her wee, the lacking object is situated as castration, which she is trying to avoid by identifying with her shooting father.

The game of killing and hiding with a Winnicott who is almost dead (Winnicott insists on his own approaching death) enacts the dead father who returns with his law of castration. Gabrielle constructs a Winnicott who says 'No' (even when he does not, as when she says to her mother that Winnicott had said 'No' to her climbing on her father's body). She has also made a dustbin-Winnicott. He is as if dead, and this dead father is the symbolic father, the father who cannot die, eternal. But the analyst is the waste product of the analysis. And Winnicott in this case writes his own death as well as the end of an analysis. The dropped object of the end of the analysis was coinciding with his own end.

9

Klein's Narrative

We saw in the last chapter how the phobic reveals that *anxiety is not without an object*. But which one? With little Hans, Freud had to interpret the meaning of this object, the horse. Whether Freud was right or wrong in making the horse the Oedipal castrating father was not so much the point as the fact that Freud gave this imaginary horse a meaning. He did so by introducing the Oedipal myth. The horse functioned as movement, a potential carrier of new meanings: the horse which had fallen, the giraffe which got crumpled are set into motion again by analysis and, therefore, changed.

We will see also how in Melanie Klein's narrative of the analysis of nine-year-old Richard (1961), the phobic object was represented, as it was for Piggle, in one of the child's nightmares. But the black island inhabited by dead and black creatures terrified less for its blackness than for its stillness. It was a spell which Richard broke by suddenly calling out 'Ahoy there'. This uncanny stillness reminds one of the Wolf-man's perturbing dream of the still wolves.

In Piggle too we have a phobia, not of any particular external object, but of her own 'awake' nightmares. We have seen that she was a step closer to adult anxiety, which is the fear of inner dangers rather than of external ones. In fact Piggle feared the productions of her own unconscious. The black mummy and the babacar appeared to her out of darkness.

The fear of the dark, so common among children, is always fear of things which appear in the dark, uncanny things, things which should not be there. The phobic object is a presence appearing against a background of absence. For Winnicott, playing was fundamental in releasing the anxiety which got stuck in the symptom.

Playing is pretending that what is absent is present; it allows a presence which would otherwise be terrifying. But play for Winnicott is also a means to allow the nascent unconscious to be verbalized. By enacting Piggle's unconscious phantasies he engaged her in a dialogue through which the unconscious could communicate.

Even though they are theoretically played down by both Klein and Winnicott, speech and the articulation of unconscious phenomena are of fundamental clinical importance to them both. Melanie Klein made a point with Richard of giving a name, which he did not know, to things like genitals, faeces and sexual intercourse. Naming, like playing, evokes an absence; it is an 'as if it were present'.

It was Melanie Klein who invented the play technique, which Winnicott later developed in his particular way. Klein, too, used play as a technique for the enactment of unconscious phantasies. But the real aim of these enactments is their verbalization. Whereas in Winnicott the unconscious emerges through a ludic dialogue, in Klein the unconscious is injected through the interpretation. This is what Lacan calls her 'injection of the symbolic'. Let us try to see what this means.

Freud did something similar with Hans when he told him the Oedipal story in the form of a fairy tale. Both Winnicott and Klein, despite their claims that they are working with infantile and pre-verbal stages of development, cannot help interpreting the unconscious phantasies of these children in Oedipal terms. Even when their interpretations unfold variations of earlier traces of Oedipal conflicts, the tragedy of Oedipus is the core of their interpretations, the structure underlying all early, classically pre-Oedipal phantasies. It becomes, in fact, difficult to disentangle the phantasy from the interpretation. In reading Klein's *Narrative*, at a certain point Richard's speech becomes an echo to the Kleinian phantasmagorical speech.

So even when Richard regressed analytically to the earliest oral and anal anxieties and phantasies, he could never escape the tragic dilemma of there being at least three in the world, instead of two. The empire of the maternal body which Richard drew for Mrs Klein had to be shared with at least one rival, first daddy, but then gradually a wider and wider set of characters joining in this world *in nuce*: his brother Paul, the dog Bobby, the canaries, cook, nurse, and at last crowds, heaps of babies, dead and alive ones. The latter constitute his phobic object: his main symptom is fear of children.

Melanie Klein's interpretative work functions as a knot which selectively structures the patient's unbound phantasies. She tries to use the Oedipal knot for earlier and earlier stages, trying to give meaning to pre-Oedipal ones. She wants to articulate the pre-verbal by 'Oedipalizing' it. Her big bet is to structure and, therefore, give meaning to what precedes meaning itself. This is the Kleinian early Oedipus.

But let us look at Richard and Klein together, at what kind of dialogue she instills in him. Let us start with the first session.

> Mrs K. had prepared some little toys and a writing pad, pencils, and chalks on the table, with two chairs by it. When she sat down, Richard also sat down, paying no attention to the toys and *looking at her in an expectant and eager way, obviously waiting for her to say something. She suggested that he knew why he was coming to her;* he had some difficulties with which he wanted to be helped. Richard agreed and at once began to talk about his worries. He was afraid of boys he met in the street and of going out by himself, and this fear had been getting worse and worse. It had made him hate school. He also thought much about the war. *Of course he knew the Allies were going to win* and was not worried, but was it not awful what Hitler did to people, particularly the terrible things he did to the Poles? Did he mean to do the same over here? But he, Richard, felt confident that Hitler would be beaten. (When speaking about Hitler, he went to have a look at a large map hanging on the wall.) (Klein, 1961, p. 19: my italics)

He waits for her to give all this a possible dialogue, silently and expectantly. She responds to it by articulating for Richard his demand of analysis.

Richard's first entry into the dialogue is an agreement, followed by the spelling out of his 'worries', his symptoms as it were: his fear of children has provoked in him a hatred of school and a fear of going out by himself. It is a fear of public places. We would define it as a perfect agoraphobia: a fear of the world at large. This world is well represented by his second 'worry': the war.

Klein interprets his worries about the war according to Oedipal parameters: conflict and rivalry with the Hitler/father. But this is not what Richard is saying. He is not worried about Britain (or himself) losing the war; *of course* he knows the Allies are going to win and Hitler to be beaten. But what really worries him is that an awful character like Hitler can exist and cause so much sorrow to humanity. Is he denying the conflict? I do not think so; he is not denying the dangers and the hate he feels for Hitler, but he seems to be stating that if he is not worried about losing the war it is because the victory is already his own.

This 'of course', this certainty, seems to be the key to his problem; that he is victorious in relation to the father and not, as Melanie Klein thought, worried about the victory of the father. He is worried that a father/Hitler can exist at all. The war brings in the *possibility* of the Oedipal conflict, the war that founds civilization, for Richard. It is not that something is wrong because of Oedipus, but rather that Oedipus tackles the problem. Similarly, we came to the conclusion that if something was wrong with Hans and Piggle it was because something went wrong *with* Oedipus and not *because* of it. In both cases we could see how the element which did not fall into its Oedipal place was precisely the father. This means that phobia in children is not an excessive reaction to the unavoidable intrusion of the father or his representative as a third term (babies), but results from the lack of such an interfering function. The father does not accomplish his symbolic role; whether he is a good enough father in other ways does not matter.

Richard differs from both Hans and Piggle in that their conflict was produced not by the war, but by a more common, traumatic event; the birth of a sister. The dual symbiotic relation to the mother, or to the father as in the case of Piggle, had been put in question not by the Oedipal triangle but by another child, who took on the role of the third term, a separating function. But what about Richard, who, on the contrary, is the last child and did not go through the experience of the birth of a sibling? Would it seem too far-fetched to say that his fear of children might be connected to the lack of a traumatic experience in relation to his possession of his mother? In Richard's case we can see how the war plays the role of the traumatic event. Richard can see the possibility of a conflict only out there, in the world war.

Klein tries to transfer this external conflict inside Richard and moves it into the transference. She is trying to make Richard take on a conflict he cannot quite put his finger on. Klein has to inject him with the Oedipal trauma.

At night he might have been afraid that when his parents went to bed something could happen between them with their genitals that would injure Mummy.

Richard looked surprised and frightened. He did not seem to understand what the word 'genital' meant. Up to this point he had obviously understood and had listened with mixed feelings.

Mrs K. asked whether he knew what she meant by 'genital'. Richard first said no, then he admitted that he thought he knew (consciously he seemed to have no conception of sexual intercourse, nor a name for the genitals). He went on to say that Daddy was very nice, very kind, he wouldn't do anything to Mummy. (Klein, 1961, p. 21)

It is striking how Richard responds to Mrs Klein, with surprise and not with a denial. He seems to ignore something, the name of the genitals and the idea of intercourse. He seems to have genuinely missed their meaning and function together with their names. The danger comes from outside: the tramp or the war that breaks in. (Remember the horse breaking into Hans's room, the bigger world breaking into the small circuit of mother and child.) It is not assumed that the real daddy will protect the mother or Richard from this danger. The father appears throughout the development of the case as a basically impotent father, a baby-father. When he was ill he was looked after like a baby, by Richard himself as well. The father becomes at that point of Richard's analysis the baby who was never born, the baby the father was not able or did not want to give to the mother. Mrs Klein interprets the tramp figure as the father, the intruder of the classical Oedipus. But could we not see in the tramp Richard himself? A tramp who is stopped not by the father but only by himself. His access to the mother appears to be too available; no law of prohibition or of separation stops Richard from his intrusion into and exhaustion of his mother. This is the third worry of Richard. He exhausts his mother with his demands.

Richard's anxiety seems to derive from this lack of boundaries, the lack of a limit which it is precisely the function of Oedipus to set. It is interesting to see how Richard reacts to his stay with the Wilson family. The Wilsons represent the disciplinary family he tolerates so badly that Klein herself infers that Richard's family must be of the tolerant kind. Strangely enough, Hans's and Piggle's families also produced a symptomatic child out of their Freudian, enlightened and tolerant upbringing in the first case and their will to be good enough parents in the second. Each case probably represents the symptom of the analyst too, as much as the child is the symptom of the parents. We have good reasons to believe that Richard's parents too had some form of acquaintance with Klein's work, because of the difficult set-up necessary for an unusual treatment. The set-up was that mother and child stayed in a hotel in *X*, away from their village in *Y*, and went back home for a day or two at weekends. This is also very telling about the family's unconscious structure: the mother and child together, even sleeping together for some of the time, undisturbed by a father who lives elsewhere.

But more interestingly, when father comes to stay in *X* for a few days, a stay which Richard was looking forward to expectantly, he fails in his role even there and then by collapsing in front of the very eyes of his son. But Klein does not want to know about this impotent father who does not give mother the baby who will separate Richard from her. She always concentrates her interpretations on his rivalry towards possible new babies. She sees Oedipus as frustrating and threatening; she hammers Richard with this imaginary castrating father who threatens him, a hating and hated father.

By this super-egoic aspect of Oedipus she tries to draw up a map of the world into which Richard can move, into which he can go to school without feeling threatened by other children as potentially dead enemies. The map of Europe which Richard looks at, turning his head upside down, is a very illuminating description of how the world is upside down for him. Klein hopes that by working through all his infantile phantasies he can make up a map where he can recognize his own psychic position in relation to the world closer to him: father, mother, brother, children, animals and so on. In other words her interpretations draw a psychic map in which Richard can make sense of his world conflict. Her map of Richard's pathological fears, the Oedipal myth she gives him (as Freud did with Hans), goes like this: you fear children because you fear your father will take your mother away and your rage will kill father as well as mother, who will be left without father at the mercy of Richard, who attacks her body in order to kill all the rival unborn babies she contains because of his envy towards her goodness (her good breast), because of mother's alliance with father and other babies.

Klein's analytical strategy is that the awareness of those split-bad parts of him, and of his schizo-paranoid stage, should push him into a new stage, the depressive one, where the realization of his good object having been split and attacked by his envy and jealousy will raise the urge to repair them, to make of split objects whole objects. But however much and well they get sewn up by the reparative effects of the depressive stage or of the analysis, the object is nevertheless irremediably split (see chapter 4). It has always two sides to it, which reparation only puts together but cannot make One. The crack remains even under the best gloss. The depressive stage is the realization that the object is split indeed.

How is it possible to reconcile the child to an Oedipal situation where he is destined to be the loser whether he loses his mother or whether he wins over the father? His victory will be achieved only at the cost of killing the father and destroying everything, with the consequence that he will end up blind like Oedipus, and devoured by guilt. The mythical Oedipus was, of course, somebody for whom the Oedipal complex failed, where the father actually dropped to the ground under his son's armed hand and where he possessed his mother and gave her children, somebody for whom the total *jouissance* of the desired object was accomplished whether he knew what he was doing or not.

That something is unknown, unconscious, does not change its tragic effects. So the problem for psychoanalysis is how to avoid the disastrous effects of incestuous love and hate inscribed in the analytical paradigm. I have tried to show how even Klein, in spite of her recourse to the breast as a good object, as the object which establishes the power of love for the mother over the power of hate towards the father, has to map all Richard's passions and phantasies within the Oedipal schema. But then one wonders why an internalization of a good breast should smooth down the Oedipal conflict, rather than having the disastrous consequences that it had with Oedipus. Is not the possession of the maternal object always secured in a conflict with rivals? Klein seems to rely on the fact that love will triumph over hate, life drive over death drive, when the two are put together in the reparative operation following the depressive stage. But how does it happen? How can love triumph over hate, and does one exist without the other? In chapter 3, we discovered this realm of passions and the devouring and cruel phantasies attached to them: how, in this realm, can the analyst find her/his instrument of work? Can one get out of their destructive effects without finding a distance from them, making a separation indeed?

Meltzer comes to our aid in identifying this problem. He is more attentive to the father's illness than is Klein. Richard responds to his father's illness with little emotion, half-listening to Klein's interpretations, responding to them by handling a penknife and putting it on his teeth. Meltzer spots the knife as a suicidal instrument; in fact Klein herself had to warn Richard against the danger. Around that time he tells his mother that if the allies lose the war he will kill himself. What kind of father does he want to save here with his own death – the Hitler/father or another kind of father, one which is as necessary to the child's psychic survival as the mother was in an earlier stage? Let us quote from the session where the Oedipal solution of Richard is magnificently illustrated.

Richard had during the last few minutes played with Mrs K.'s umbrella, which he had opened. He made it spin round and said he liked it. Then he used it as a parachute with which he was supposed to float down. He looked at the trade mark and stated with satisfaction that it was British made. Then, again holding it open, he turned round and round with it and said that he was dizzy, he did not know where it was taking him. He also said over and over again that 'the whole world is turning round'. Then he let the umbrella drop gently; he once more said it was a parachute and that he was not sure whether it would go down the right way. He told Mrs K. that he had completely wrecked Mummy's best umbrella when he used it on a windy day. She had been 'speechless with rage'.

Mrs K. interpreted the umbrella as her breast; that it was British made meant it was a good breast, and that Mummy's breast was good too. She referred to his doubts about what Mrs K. contained – a good or a bad Mr K. The open umbrella stood for the breast, but the stick in it stood for Mr K.'s genital. Richard did not know whether he could trust this breast when he took it in because it was mixed with Mr K.'s genital, just as in his mind his parents and their genitals were mixed inside him. The question where the umbrella would take him expressed his uncertainty whether they were controlling him inside or not. The world which was turning round was the world he had taken into himself when he took in the breast – or rather Mummy mixed with Daddy, and her children, and all she contained. He felt the internalized powerful Daddy-penis – the secret weapon – as something which made him powerful if he used it against an external enemy. But it became dangerous if it attacked and controlled him internally. Nevertheless, he trusted Mummy and Daddy – the umbrella – more than previously, both as external people and inside him. That was also why he now treated Mrs K.'s umbrella more carefully than he had formerly treated Mummy's. (Klein, 1961, pp. 455–6)

Here, although the good breast seems to take all the credit for Richard's improvements, the central role of the paternal phallus, the umbrella stick, is as much evident as it is played down. Meltzer argues: 'But surely the umbrella would not function at all without the central stick-penis' (1978, p. 120). He can see that the umbrella works and the world turns around in the right direction only because there is a stick at the centre which supports it. And this is for Lacan not the imaginary father who prohibits and enjoys everything (the horde's primal father) but a symbolic father, the one who by coming in the way of mother and child offers a law which makes the world move and not get stuck within the round surface of the mother's breast. The child grows out of his/her infancy only if a new world is offered to him/her, a wider circuit than the maternal one. In Richard's case, the father having failed (collapsed), it is the war which has brought in the wider symbolic world.

The stick is what Lacan calls the function of the phallus. This is the function by which the father, from being an intruder, becomes a donor, the carrier of a gift. In the case of Richard the expected gift is that of sexual potency, the possibility of being able to turn from his stuckness with his mother, which did not even allow him to go to school, to the possibility of loving and making love to another woman, thanks to the mediation of a father with whom he can identify as the carrier of the phallus (rather than being one for mother).

What is striking in Klein's construction of infantile development is the fact that the earlier we trace it, the more frightful and persecutory our relation to the object becomes. And so it is for Lacan too, even though from a different angle and with different theoretical and clinical applications. Why, therefore, is such a primordial object so basically bad? Lacan would answer, unlike Klein who assumed an infantile omnipotence, that this primordial relation with the mother is based on a total dependence of the infant on the mother's omnipotence. The effects of a prematuration of birth as a loss of oneself and the reciprocal and devouring desire of mother/

child, although unbearable, is ensnaring because of the illusion that nothing is left to be desired; the world at large is only an unwelcome intruder to resist. This is neurosis, which so often announces itself in childhood as phobia.

But why a children phobia in Richard's case? Would I agree with Klein's theoretical explanation that the basic cause of any psychic disturbance and therefore of the case in question is innate envy and greed? Envy and greed are ultimately for Klein the innate cause of anxiety and of the early schizo-paranoid phantasies which go with it. Winnicott certainly found this innatistic solution unacceptable. But we know that for Winnicott the world is good and primarily the breast which feeds us. It is up to humans to be good enough, to be up to it, as it were. Why this breast does not seem that good to most of his patients is not answered. That this breast might not be good enough for man's desire has never occurred to Winnicott. Klein is a little closer to the concept of desire in giving a theoretical and clinical weight to the degenerations of desire that envy (*avoir envie* in French means also to feel like, to want) and greed seem to represent. Greed and envy, on which Klein put so much stress, are not simple excesses of a degenerate desire, its bad aspects, as it were, but the result of the avoidance of it. They are stuck desire, which is not working, and does not move the subject. Not by chance, in all three cases the little patients are obsessed with means of transport: horses, carriages, cars, trains, buses, etc.

> Richard mentioned a dream. *He and Mrs K. had got into a bus and found that there was no conductress on it and that the bus was empty. There was also a car in which there were some people, and on the seat a little girl was lying. The car was very flat . . .*
> *It was so eerie, so ghostly. The bus slowed down when he rang the bell and Richard jumped out while it was still moving. He was glad that Mrs Wilson was standing there and took him to her house. The people in the car reminded him of some people who stayed at the hotel . . .*
> The little girl would then represent a sister whom he might want to have . . . During this session Richard had scarcely paid attention to passers-by. He looked very unhappy. Once or twice he put his head on his arm on the table and appeared as if he did not know what to do with himself. His wish to be caressed and cuddled by Mrs K. was very obvious. (Klein, 1961, pp. 449, 452, 453: Klein's italics)

Richard tells her this final dream as a heart-breaking goodbye. What has changed from the starting position of the first dream? The girl he had not been and he did not have as a sister appears in his dream but, unlike in the first dream, she is not part of his phobia. He does not fear any more his desire of other children (he does not pay attention to the passers-by); he has brought the child, lying down or dead, into his unconscious. It has become meaningful, rather than a senseless symptom. The feared child finds an accommodation in the family drive (car) but still as a dead one, 'eerie', 'ghostly', 'flat'. But, most of all, the dream shows a fundamental shift in his means of transport. Even though the bus which has transported him to Mrs Klein throughout his analysis is empty (analysis over), he can still walk. By walking, he can establish his distance from what in Lacanian terms is called a 'fundamental phantasy', represented by the funerary car of his parents' desire. Klein has given him not a solution to this deadly sterility but other means of transport, the possibility of going, at least in the future, to a new home with another woman. The promise is suspended until a future date.

Part IV

Part IV

10

To Die of Shame

According to Freud, shame, disgust and morality are the three primary repressive forces which act as resistances against sexual drives (1905b). Freud describes disgust as a protection against the polymorphous perversity of childhood; morality is also an inner counterforce, but more directly connected to an external force, namely, to social authority.

Shame is a force which dictates modesty, a covering up or a veiling of the obscene. But how to define the obscene with which shame is concerned? Is it an internal or external force we protect ourselves against with shame? We have to take into account that Freud considered these three repressive forces as primary and not pathological in the way that guilt and anxiety are. On the contrary, they are dams which restrain sexual development within those limits which are regarded as normal.

Freud explained them as historical precipitates of inhibitions to which the sexual drive has been subjected during the psychogenesis of the human race. Therefore they are effects of repression, but a primary or in-built one. It is worth noting that, according to Freud, it is an original restriction of sexuality which paves the way to sublimation and civilization. These dams arise when upbringing and external influences give a signal, but they, morality included, are not caused by such external influences, which have the sole function of signalling for the inner forces to start to operate. So their relation to repression proper is a subtle one. On the one hand they are the matrix of any future possible neurotic repression (they determine the human privilege of a biological predisposition to neurosis); on the other hand, if they predispose to neurosis, they are not it.

Repression is not neurosis; on the contrary, Freud thought that the neurotic is someone who represses badly. One could go so far as to assume that they may constitute an original possibility of a biological repressive norm of which neurotic repression is a deviation or its degeneration.

We might outline the hypothesis that shame is the primordial response to the obscene. It entails an act of veiling or covering, rather than (neurotic) denying, (perverse) disavowing and (psychotic) foreclosing. If we pursue this perspective, neurotic repression will be, then, a false or failed act of covering whose effect is not shame but guilt and anxiety.

Let us first follow Freud in some descriptions of unconscious phenomena which entail shame: slips of the tongue, jokes, typical dreams of being naked, and the phantasy of 'A child is being beaten' in an attempt to characterize shame and the obscene.

Slips of the tongue raise a sense of shame as they uncover an intention to insult or an inward contempt, or expose an inner insincerity. It is a self-betrayal which imposes a recognition of inner motives. This explains why a slip of the tongue in analysis is always welcome; it imposes admission and therefore it is rarely contested. Thereby it imposes a shame which cannot be denied; it belongs to the subject and it is often welcome by him/her too, in so far as there is a relief at the fact that a wish which was impossible to say has slipped out all by itself. The sense of the comic which ensues turns shame into pleasure.

It is also pleasure that a good joke provokes. It seems that it is by this interplay of shame and pleasure that guilt is evaded. Slips and jokes are at the limit of modesty where they uncover (without provoking) guilt and anxiety. Furthermore, what is most puzzling is the fact that this uncovering provokes a pleasurable frankness, which contrasts sharply with the excruciating feelings related to neurotic repression. Honesty seems to be the only force which can beat the force of shame.

But the Freudian key text on shame is in the 'Interpretation of dreams', essentially, of the embarrassing dreams of being naked. To quote Freud:

> Dreams of being naked or insufficiently dressed in the presence of strangers sometimes occur with the additional feature of there being a complete absence of any such feeling as shame on the dreamer's

part. We are only concerned here, however, with those dreams of being naked in which one does feel shame and embarrassment and tries to escape or hide, and is then overcome by a strange inhibition which prevents one from moving and makes one feel incapable of altering one's distressing situation. It is only with this accompaniment that the dream is typical . . . Its essence lies in *a distressing feeling in the nature of shame* and in the fact that one wishes to hide one's own nakedness, as a rule by locomotion, but finds one is unable to do so. I believe the great majority of my readers will have found themselves in this situation in dreams.

The nature of the undressing involved is customarily far from clear. The dreamer may say 'I was in my chemise', but this is rarely a distinct picture. The kind of 'undress' is usually so vague that the description is expressed as an alternative: 'I was in my chemise or petticoat.' As a rule the defect in the dreamer's toilet is not so grave as to appear to justify the shame to which it gives rise. In the case of a man who has worn the Emperor's uniform, nakedness is often replaced by some breach of the dress regulations: 'I was walking in the street without my sabre and saw some officers coming up', or 'I was without my necktie', or 'I was wearing civilian check trousers', and so on. The people in whose presence one feels ashamed are almost always strangers, with the features left indeterminate. In the typical dream it never happens that the clothing which causes one so much embarrassment is objected to, or so much as noticed, by the onlookers. On the contrary, they adopt an indifferent or . . . solemn and stiff expression of face. This is a suggestive point.

The embarrassment of the dreamer and the indifference of the onlookers offer us, when taken together, a contradiction of the kind that is so common in dreams. (Freud, 1905c, pp. 242–3: my italics)

In order to interpret these dreams, Freud has to resort to the literary form of fairy tales, just as this typical dream has something to do with childhood. The story he refers to is Hans Anderson's 'The emperor's new clothes', where two impostors claim that the garment they have woven for the emperor is visible only to virtuous and honest people. Hence everybody, namely, the emperor and the crowd in front of which he walks, pretends not to notice his nakedness, until a child in the crowd cries out, 'Look, the emperor has no clothes on!' Thereby the emperor is equivalent to the dreamer in the place of a child who is seen inadequately dressed and without shame.

The dream refers to a time in childhood when polymorphous perversity and exhibitionism were possible, a time which resembles that mythical time when the expulsion from Paradise had not yet

wakened shame and anxiety. So the dream's wish-fulfilment requires exhibiting to proceed while censorship demands it shall be
stopped. This is the shame which belongs only to the dreamer, who
alone sees his nakedness, whereas the others, the onlookers or the
crowd in front of the naked emperor, do not notice or rather pretend
they do not notice, as they are covering up indecency and shame on
the dreamer's part. Freud says the dream is the impostor, for it hides
the subject's exhibitionism with the blindness of the crowd.

Freud uses both words, 'shame' and 'embarrassment' (*Scham* and
Verlegenheit), but what he is referring to is 'a distressing feeling in
the nature of shame'. We should distinguish shame from embarrassment, the latter being the conscious feeling of having been found
out by the other, whereas shame is the encounter of the subject with
the veil which covers and points out his/her nakedness. Thereupon
this 'feeling of the nature of shame' seems to be something in between shame and embarrassment, as it appears only on the side of
the dreamer, while the onlookers represent his/her repression of the
truth of nakedness as well as his/her will to exhibit. The evasion of
an inner shame gives in to embarrassment *vis-à-vis* the other. But the
dream shows also that only the dreamer, who is at heart a child
without shame, can see it. This kind of dream shows both shame
and its opposite, exhibitionism; it shows veiling and unveiling as
condensed in one action; it shows both modesty at wanting to
remove nakedness and inhibition of movement, an unwillingness to
remove it. But these typical dreams also lead us further into our
investigation of the obscene.

Freud interprets shame psycho-genetically. Shame arose when
human beings stood upright from being on all fours, and thus the
genitals needed protection from exposure. After that, vision took
over from smell in sexuality. For Freud, philogenesis could explain
the apparently pre-programmed response to certain signals which
are given by external influences and education. Before those signals
are given the child does not know shame, as s/he has not as yet
eaten the apple of true knowledge. Nakedness is children's innocence while knowledge is about covering their genitals. It is common understanding that innocence is not lost with the revelation
of the facts of life. On the contrary, it is lost when an injunction
to cover oneself is addressed to the subject (plate 6): when the
Oedipal prohibition against incest is signalled. Without this inter-

diction there is no shame. That is why early sexual seduction, whether passive (hysteria) or active (obsessional neurosis), undoes the work of shame and diminishes the child's educability, because the child remains in Paradise, we could say. This is the paradox of child abuse.

In Freud's case of the Wolf-man we have an example of shame. The Wolf-man emptied his bladder in front of a servant girl, whose name was (you can guess) Matrona, around the time of the primal scene. This shameful servant's name covered his desires towards mother and sister, as well as his revengeful wish to debase them. It was at the recognition of this shameful feeling that repression was lifted at this point of analysis.

If guilt is a suffering from a hidden source, shame is a covering of what is otherwise seen. It reveals what it covers. Guilt is linked to anxiety instead. Unlike shame, guilty anxiety signals a danger of something which cannot be looked at; it signals the fear that the repressed will return. The repressed is dangerous because it consists of a desire which could cost the other's love.

Guilt, therefore, stems from anxiety about this loss. I have shown how for Freud the difference between phobia and anxiety is that the first elects an object as the source of fear, whereas anxiety is without an obvious object; it is an alarm ringing at any approach of the dangerous, repressed object. We have seen in the previous cases that phobic anxiety is the fear of a presence in a background of absence. We can witness here one of Lacan's typical ways of thinking, where absence takes on a positive or operational function in our psychic structure. As we just said, we repress a desire which would cost us love, but repressing does not mean losing. On the contrary, repression is a secret preserving of the object of shame, always obscenely available in the unconscious. It is a form of cheating on an authority who, at any time, can find out your shameful secret. Anxiety gives the signal of danger to this authority, the internalized authority of the super-ego.

This is the double-edged paradox of a secondary repression: it keeps the repressed instinct functioning in conflict not with an external authority, but with the internalized authority of the super-ego. That is why the more we repress the more we feel guilty.

Freud gives the example of the strict super-ego of the saints. It is produced by the repressed intention to sin, which cannot be hidden from God. Guilt, unlike shame, never succeeds in covering. It is, rather, the failure in covering. We feel the force of repression feeding the force of the super-ego as guilt.

The super-ego is an imaginary authority based on renounced aggressiveness against the loved and hated authority of the Other. It is a revolt against it. Guilt is, in fact, what characterizes obsessional ambivalence and the melancholic's shameless self-reproaches. We can see the difference from remorse, which bears on a real misdeed, whereas guilt is the effect which goes with a repressed desire.

But it is with shame that we enter into the realm of Lacanian practice: that is, into the realm of the symbolic. We will see how shame is the primary response of the subject to the Other's verbal utterance, as these words both split the subject from this Other and, therefore, split the subject within itself. Shame veils this very splitting by coming to be in the place of the lost Other. This veiling (primary repression) keeps the object of desire out of sight, but not out of desire.

I noted that Freud saw shame as the effect of a change of position, as with a child who has just learned to stand on its feet. Upright, one sees new things, gets new messages, makes new conquests and endures new losses. Upright, one shares the world of upright people and their laws; the message changes from the primary maternal injunction, 'Eat, suck and show yourself to me', into the Oedipal injunction, 'Cover yourself, your greed and your desire for me.' Language starts with this lost Garden of Eden, with the injunction not to eat the apple of knowledge. It starts with this signal which sets out disobedience, shame and modesty.

We have seen how Hans was upright, ready to identify with his father's insignia, but no message, no signal arrived. He could fully enjoy his mother in bed: there was no injunction from the father, no words of prohibition to bar him. Hans himself tried to institute a prohibition in the form of a phobia, as did Klein's Richard. This phobia is tied to our imaginary father, who shares the pre-Oedipal, arbitrary, dual law of the mother rather than the ministry of the social bond that the law is.

Shame is introduced by the symbolic father, the one who makes the son urinate with modesty, who gives his penis a meaning: an identification with the father that gives the child the insignia of virility, on a penis which had functioned so far as being an instrument of polymorphous perverse enjoyment. At this point Hans's penis comes to represent the phallus, a gift given by the father on the condition that it will be decently covered. Shame is, then, concerned with an acknowledged cover-up rather than with disavowal (which is the device of perversion, the most shameless disturbance). The core of the obscene is covered, and kept at the same time in the *Aufhebung*[1] through shame. But what is this fundamental obscenity, this structural cover-up? Both in the embarrassing dreams and in the story of the naked emperor, the others, the crowd, by not noticing nakedness, are covering up the naked truth. A fig leaf was sufficient to cover the site where our desires do not coincide with the desires of God; it covered the nakedness of Paradise.

As well, in the embarrassing dreams, nakedness is vague. Like the fig leaf, ties or chemises are covering as well as phallic attributes. Could we deduce from this that the function of the phallus has to do with covering? Or that the dress itself is a phallic attribute which covers? And is this in contradiction to the Lacanian notion that the phallus can exercise its function only when veiled? Or, like ties and collars, is the phallus a veil in itself?

In his paper on the signification of the phallus, Lacan writes: 'Phallus is a signifier whose function, in the intra-subjective economy of the analysis, lifts the veil perhaps from the function it performed in the mysteries' (1977e, p. 285).[2] The Villa of the Mysteries is all about unveiling; it unveils the ecstasy of the god lying across the lap of a woman (the father in a feminine enjoyment, separate from the veiled phallus in the next scene), and next, the demon of shame, Aidos, who whips a woman placed near the glorious nudity of a dancer. The whip and the veil mask the appearance of the phallus on the scene of nakedness, in the place of 'nothing on', of the lack of phallus which appears in its essence of *simulacrum*: something with the appearance of a deity, but only the appearance.

The frescos we toured at the beginning of this book now have clearer outlines. They represent initiatory rites whose function was precisely to unveil a god off-duty, non-erect, in an ecstatic and indecent rest. They unveil the feminine enjoyment of god, even infantile enjoyment on the mother's lap.

These frescos are what is left of the mysteric rites. Their artistic function is not far from one of the functions of psychoanalysis: the function of interpretation. Is not the analytical interpretation, like the artistic interpretation, too, a veil which unveils? Is not the interpretation too supposed to be revelatory and ambiguous at the same time?

Derrida, commenting on analytical interpretation in *The Postcard* (1987), defined it as 'an undressing which dresses' or 'a dress which undresses'. I think that most analysts would agree with Freud that the problem of exposure and inadequate clothing typically arises in analysis, especially through dreams. An analysand of mine used to complain about feeling very vulnerable, very exposed in her analysis, while dreaming a lot that she was poorly dressed. Then one day, she dreamt that she had undressed herself and stolen some of her analyst's clothing. This dream uncovered both her will to exhibit (mainly to herself, a desire to see by showing to the other) and her will to get covered and rehabilitated by the other (possibly without having to pay for it) by stealing my clothes. That clothes stand also for interpretations to wear for the occasion was shown by a case I had in supervision. She was a bisexual woman who was very alert to any sign of possible homophobia on her analyst's part. Once her analyst had interpreted some of her dreams in terms of some classical Oedipal ambivalence. In the following session the analysand related a dream in which all she could find for herself in a clothes shop was a ready-made dress on its hanger.

The phallus, then, like the clothes woven by the impostors who make one believe one is dressed, dresses nothing, or the emperor's lack of honesty. Like the emperor, one appears 'as if' one had clothes on. One appears as if one had the phallus, but in reality one wears only a simulacrum: something which looks as if it were it. Women have to hide the lack that they represent behind beautiful clothes. But men have to get dressed too, for they have to look as if they have the phallus. But at the end of the day they have only a penis, which can be as naked and off-duty as anything else.

My equation is: obscene = naked = lack. But what is the truth of this lack which horrifies us all? If it were only a question of anatomical lack we could not explain why men are affected by it as much as women. But if we consider that being naked represents vulnerability, the exposure of one's own secret weakness, then having clothes on gives one back one's human identity and dignity. In the same way the phallus represents mastery and sexual identity, which make up for a tiny bit of the cost of castration, being cast out of the lost paradise of our unconditional enjoyment of the mother. Truth is, therefore, this undressing which reveals a lack of being, or lack of that Dionysus-bit of us, which is at the mercy of its ecstatic enjoyment.

But now a question could be asked: what is this mastery for? Is it a struggle of pure prestige, to put it in a Hegelian way? Or is it a purely defensive struggle for life? Drives for mastery and for self-preservation are, for Freud, new channels into which the original instinct for cruelty is directed. This instinct accounts for later sadism/masochism (something akin to Klein's schizo-paranoid stage). But Lacan, like Klein, considers these early destructive phenomena as indicators of an even more radical drive: the death drive.

At the beginning of this book I said that death, together with sexuality, are the fundamental inner forces to be countered, whether in a neurotic way or not, by our psychic set-up. Death needs covering as much as sexuality does. The recognition of an irreducible death drive is a difficult task. Some analysts like to deny it. One is Winnicott (even though in his practice he works with the death drive, as we have seen in his case of the Piggle). According to Lacan, the death drive is a fundamentally radical character in repetition which insists and characterizes the human psychic reality. We could say, then, that what shines forth behind the veils of modesty, which the neurotic does not want even to look at, is the ultimate lack of being, death itself.

Lacan concludes his seminar *L'envers de la psychanalyse* (1991b) with the chapter entitled 'To die of shame'. In this seminar he shifts shame from the field of sexuality to the side of death. So this 'Dying of shame' is not shame as such. It is the relation of shame to death. The neurotic would rather die than feel shame! This is shown in another dream Freud dwells on, one where the dreamer's father (who had just died) appeared in the dream as having died without knowing it. But Freud adds to the 'having died': 'as the dreamer wished . . . how terrible it would have been if his father had had any suspicion of it' (1911a, p. 225). Dying of shame is thus repressed shame; it is guilt for the subject's flight from the encounter with shame.

The encounter with the repressed which analysis makes possible opens a passage from repressed guilt to shame. In analysis the task for the neurotic is to reverse his/her position in relation to death. The neurotic thinks that the cause of one's shame must warrant death; neurotic illness is a struggle to counteract this death drive. It does not cover it with decency, but keeps it raw, always ready to pop out of the cupboard as a naked skeleton.

That is why the neurotic is always cheating on death, obsessed with it indeed. In this way the neurotic tries to be the master of his/her own death, believing that s/he is the agent of it, and that death is deeply deserved.

But as this death on command does not happen, the analysand is left, then, with a shameful life to gulp down. Because even the neurotic knows that life, whether shameful or not, does not deserve death, which does not have other masters than itself. The neurotic subject, thereby, by wanting to master death is fighting against it, and does not recognize it as the ultimate master, whereas dying of shame positions the subject as a being against death (against the shame which goes with it). Shame, without dying, positions us as being for death. Life deserves shame; we do not deserve to die from it. We carry on in spite of our shameful lack of being, in spite of broken ideals and identifications, in spite of our psychic, historical, family determinations, in spite of our mortality. Dying of shame is the reverse of psychoanalysis. For psychoanalysis, Lacan says, shames you into living.

Psychoanalysis uncovers a limit beyond which we cannot go even though we would like to. In both cases, either because of an infringement or because of a limitation, shame covers and points at a hole in the core of our moral wholeness. This is the analytical truth which makes us shameful, but not dead. The only thing left to be done is to endorse it. It is not easy, though, because truth, as it operates in the analytical process, is not a clear-cut, transparent and whole truth. On the contrary, it appears and disappears through little gaps of consciousness, from a slip of the tongue, a dream, a forgotten word, a missed action. It appears fleetingly in tears in our well-dressed conscious discourse; a bare piece of flesh appears and gets covered again. It appears for a moment, and for a moment makes you almost die of shame, but it does not last.

Truth is not a faithful lover but a seducer which no one can marry; it always abandons you, slips away and covers itself again. Those readers who are analysts know this phenomenon very well; in fact this appearing and disappearing is the very movement of the unconscious, which opens and closes up again. It pulsates like a heart. The analyst 'lifts a shadow', to quote Lacan again, and 'finds carrion'; that is, 'he finds a beyond the limit (the Real) which is not made to be known'.[3] Certainly knowledge, whether psychoanalytical or academic, can be added to the 'real' precisely like a dress; it can shape, veil and give relief to it, but does not replace it. Conscious knowledge, even if it is psychoanalytical, will always reflect language, the shadow falling over the obscenity of truth. Conversely, the truth which is unveiled in analysis has the effect of a fall from knowledge, an exposure which, even though only for a moment, produces something new in the relation between conscious and unconscious, knowledge and truth, life and death, love and hate.

So psychoanalysis does not produce truth, which is unknowable even to the analyst, but it is from its fleeting exposures that a friction in our psychic system takes place, which produces a sparkle of . . . desire indeed. For Lacan this sparkle is a potentially revolutionary fire: it puts in question our relation to our previous knowledge, which, like the emperor's clothes, even when it is invisible, serves mastery. Knowledge serves mastery by dressing up its shame, and fixed knowledge is the authority which weighs on and blinds us to our truth. The original master must have been somebody who pushed himself forward out of shame, pretending that 'he knew' that he was dressed, even though he was not. According to Freud, the thirst for knowledge derives from sublimated sexual curiosity diverted into cultural channels. But it may be more correct to say that knowledge counteracts sexual curiosity, to cover the shame of its truth. Analysis exposes the lack in our masters of knowledge, reveals that they are born out of this shame which we all feel because of our division and partiality. In analysis we realize our dependence on the other. This dependence was masked by a slavery to false and reassuring masters, super-egoic and ideal ones. By stripping one of its masters, psychoanalysis points at a shameful dependence. As we have said, the master is the one who covers this dependence out of shame. But what does this nakedness produce in analysis? The possibility to cover it anew. We do not seem to be able to see the world except when a veil is placed in the way. As Derrida says, this undressing dresses. We cannot escape clothes. But we can change them, invent new ones, as the cowl makes the monk, and the red shoes the dancer. Analysis undresses, then, an empty place (emptied of imaginary masters) which the analysand has to dress up again with modesty.

Penelope

She was always busy working, doing hundreds of things compulsively, whatever they might be, but never completing any of them, and she could make no decision about what direction to take in her work. She could not commit herself to anything, even to a country or a place to live. She saw herself like a gypsy, came to her sessions burdened with bags, carrying her few possessions around with her. 'Being stuck' was her main complaint: she made her everyday life a torment by her hundreds of things to do, and even when she set out to do any one thing her indecision was not over. She had to decide all over again if that was the right decision after all. As a consequence of this indecision, at night she got panic attacks, insomnia and a tormenting backache: she regularly saw an osteopath who could only relieve her pain for a while. 'There is no point in going to him for my back', she said, 'if I have not worked out what causes it.' Like the Greek Penelope, she undid at night by her anxiety attacks what she had compulsively done in the day.

From the first session, she returned unceasingly to the trauma of her childhood: her mother had taken her away from their country, and from her father, to come to live in this country. Her mind constantly came back to this lost father-land which she hardly remembered but to which she had promised eternal loyalty. She was for the father against the mother who robbed her of what she called her essence, a childhood to remain faithful to; she recalled it with such intensity and freshness that she sobbed every time that she told me about it. This crying was to characterize her analysis and the problems raised in it.

So this apparently obsessional young woman, always frantically busy, with obsessional night rituals, always torn by trivial decisions, burst into hysterical tears. I did not have to say much for her mouth to run with words and her eyes with tears. At first these tears were felt by her as a revelation, precisely the hysterical core against which she was fighting. But as the scene repeated itself regularly, I noticed that although she could cry only as long as there was some speech involved from either side, after her bursting into tears my utterance was not welcome, as if it had been what made her cry. Then I started to refrain from speaking and let myself take the function of pure witness to her tears, trying to get at their meaning by neither rejecting nor encouraging them; I put myself in an analytical *time to understand*, as it were.

She had always rejected psychotherapy before, as her mother had pushed her into it quite early on. Her mother thought that Penelope was 'loony', as she had exasperated her mother by crying non-stop at the time when they moved to England. She would stop only by shutting herself in a dark room; thereby life and tears were over at the same time. Her mother's message was: you are mad and need psychotherapy. Penelope's response was to refuse therapy and cry more. Once she was in analysis her crying continued, but only when accompanied by an articulation: no, mother is mad, and I am the evidence of it. Therefore, at this point she gave me one meaning for her tears: the evidence of mother's madness.

Her relation to her mother, the way she describes it, is a constant running away from and returning to her. Penelope always works abroad for a while, starts a successful career, and then leaves it, comes back to mother to start all over again. 'If I am wrong it is my mother's responsibility', she said, 'so my life must be wrong, even if the cost is destroying myself.' It was at this point that I reminded her of one of the few memories she had of her childhood in her country; where she went into the garden shed which had been locked up for a while, and to her horror found dead birds all over the floor. She thought it had been caused by the locked door which had trapped the birds. But after having cleared the shed of all the mess she locked the door again, being perfectly aware that she was perpetuating a deadly trap. She had left it the way it was, as everything has to remain the way it was, even at the cost of death. In this memory we have the subject designated by the death drive placed in a dark room. But what about the signifier Penelope was relating to with horror?

Lacan explains that in the utterance, 'I am afraid he will not come', the subject is in the 'not', which represents the signifier as negation, as its own elision or censure.[4] What was the traumatic reality of her parents' geographical separation eliding or censoring?

A separation which had already taken place before moving to England? This became my question at this point. Her response was that she regards her mother's decision as sudden and inexplicable. I ended the session on this 'inexplicable'.

The session after that bore a further reply to my question: she did not want to know what happened between her parents, that was not her business, and she did not care, anyway. All she was concerned with was that her mother was wrong and father was right. 'But right about what?', I asked naively. Here she did not know and did not want to know. She seemed suspended on this blank in her judgement; she identified with this very blank; she called it innocence, or her essence. It seemed that the only way she could fill this gap in knowledge (her innocence) was with tears. But it was in this same session that, quite casually, a new story emerged. Her father had been taken to court by her mother for paedophilia, homosexuality and having sexually abused her elder sister; he lost by sentence of court and never came to England to see his children. (She went to visit him once, to her mother's horror, the same horror Penelope felt at the sight of the dead birds, and only after that was there some irregular correspondence between them.) This was the story she did not want to know, even after she had told me, as we are going to see.

After a few sessions she produced one of her rare dreams; it was a long dream, but worth reporting, not only because of its apparent lack of distortion and its complex transferential meaning, but also because of an important shift of vision. For the first time in her life, she said, she had dreamt in colour:

> I am walking by a lake with mother and sister, I am not sure if they were all there. In this field by the lake there were lots of people who were watching helicopters or aeroplanes taking off for somewhere all night; it was evening and in the morning a woman came back, she looked strong and I thought of myself as strong as well, I could have made it too. I really wanted to go, I really did. But I could not move, I could not do anything. Then, I was at home which I did not recognize as my own, I was in the kitchen with my sister. My mother comes in and I speak to her, I tell her everything, how much I had wished to go in the evening but I could not. She replied that my sister is so much better in these things, something my mother often says in reality. I got so upset that I shouted at her, 'You have given me such a hell . . .' My mother tensed up, her face looking really desperate and, grasping my arm, she drove her nails into it until it bled; it

wasn't violence but desperation. And then my mother said: 'Don't you know that I gave my blood to keep you alive?' I suddenly realized that my mother was right, she had given us blood to keep us alive. I started to cry as she went into the next room. I went on crying sitting on the sofa with my sister. It was such a relieving, authentic and sad cry as I have never had before. I had always cried primarily to upset my mother. But now, in the dream, I was not crying for her.

This dream had an effect of appeasement for a time; it uncovered her desire to tell her mother what she would have liked to tell her all along, but could not without making her desperate, a mother who gave her a hell of a life. This impossibility of telling her desire without hurting her mother and herself was the hell she was concerned with at this point. But this hell had overlapped with an earlier one, the one concerning her separation from a guilty and loved father, an always present and never accomplished separation.

Therefore the hopeful version of the dream could have been that analysis was given the role of promoting a mental reconciliation with her mother, whose desperation she felt guilty about, and which she recognized in the dream in her statement, 'my mother was right, she had given us blood.' A sense of shame, rather than guilt, for having failed to realize this before seemed to be the cause of her tears. It was articulated in the dream as crying for herself rather than for somebody else.

I hoped we had come to a turning point in the use of her crying in the transference. We had got rid of its super-egoic addressee in order to come closer to the gap from which sprang her tears. But this turned out to be the wrong interpretation of the dream: or rather, I was taken in by it, by its literality. I was, therefore, taken in by the very wish-fulfilment of the dream, where the wish, the egoic wish, is a *fait accompli*.

It is true that it was also a wish to get rid of this stumbling block which her clash with her mother constituted. In this, the dream did not describe a *fait accompli*, but what might be accomplishable if she could only have been strong enough to face precisely what was missing in the dream, the father towards whom the helicopters flew and from whom the strong woman came back, having survived his abuse (her 'sister was so much better in these things'). Her impossible desire resided in this 'veld of the Id' (the field by the lake in the dream) where ego and superego were 'camping' in the dream.[5] But it was only in the light of further analysis that the dream took on this new significance.

In fact her crying went on in the sessions in the structure showed by the dream: her crying on the couch (sofa in the dream) was addressed to her silent sister (silent analyst), the one who knew the father's guilt in a silence which dispatched to the subject his own intimations (whereas any verbal intervention of the analyst was contested). I had to hear, but responding was impossible, because for her it meant, 'Stop crying.' The silence of the analyst operated in two ways: (1) the wished-for silence of a sister, an alter ego; (2) making present the noisy absence of a mother who had always to be dispatched (next door in the dream) with her guilt and her melancholia, which were materialized in Penelope.

Penelope's madness was the evidence of her mother's guilt; madness was her desire, which was trapped in the task of keeping itself hidden, but was still felt as the mother's desire to abuse her children. The child abuser became the mother for her; that is, she enacted the possibility of a reversed court sentence, where her mother was to be condemned on the evidence of Penelope being 'loony'. Her crying was still a reproach to the mother and the speech of the analyst was always a super-egoic counter-reproach: 'You are wrong or mad in crying for such a shameful father.'

Her obsessional symptoms had taken, then, the place of the crying reproach in her life, and her life became a reproach to mother: her self-destruction, dying like a trapped bird, was her victory over her mother. But the memory of the dead birds unmasked to her her own responsibility for perpetuating this self-destruction, so that the early, hopeful interpretation of the dream still held. In both cases her own inner shame emerged as opposed to guilt and embarrassment, where the former is the perpetuation of an unconscious crime and its consequent punishment, and the latter the conscious feeling of having been found out by the other. Shame, on the other hand, is the encounter of the subject with the veil which covers nakedness; in other words, the encounter with the signifier of the paternal abuse. The subject takes on with modesty his/her responsibility but not the guilt related to his/her death drive (to give and take blood).

But Penelope's crying brought to bear a double demand: (1) her right to cry for an authentic grief without being considered mad by me because of it; (2) crying to exasperate the other who turned into her condemning super-ego again, so provoking guilt instead of inner shame. Her analysis unfolded between these two possibilities: a cry for help, that is, for the emergence of the suppressed signifier of paternal abuse, and a cry which suppressed the drive to liberate a *reality* (however inner, as Kleinians would have it) of an abusing mother. Psychoanalysis was not to cure her, otherwise her mother would have been right in claiming she needed it. For a while I felt in a position of complete impasse: as an analyst my function was to fail, as the utterance of 'the subject supposed to know' had taken on a super-egoic function, and upheld the possibility of a guilty sentence being truthful. So I found myself in the position where any utterance of mine turned into a reproach, into an attacking relation; and like her mother's nails in her flesh, it would have the effect of freezing her cry into a cry of spite.

Only at this point did I come to a *time to conclude*, after the time to understand which I have described earlier. The conclusion was that this analysis had to proceed 'in spite' of the analyst, and that only my religious silence would do the trick, in spite of her tears. Only by being a silent listener could I relieve her from an imaginary exchange of reciprocal exasperation and spite: as the speech of the other had a super-egoic function, for it upheld her shame. Nevertheless she had to speak if only to defend her right to cry, and, whether she liked it or not, she had to speak to another who was supposed to know the truth, in silence, like her sister. This means that her self-destructive defiance was addressed to a super-egoic mother whose law was to give and take blood. This melancholic mother had to go next door, to take a distance from her. So another aspect of the dream could be stressed only *après coup*. After the earlier stress on the articulation of her response to her mother's intimations where some of my verbal presence allowed the gradual exhaustion of the ego's utterance in an object relation to her mother, it was only in my verbal absence, in my being 'elsewhere', that she was heard in her own utterance beyond the ego-to-ego, and the ego-to-super-ego, wrestling, in the field of the id. The silence of the analyst aimed at suspending the super-egoic utterance which her tears were not able to stop, but only in order to make her hear her own defiance to blood and death shouted at, or better to say cried at, the Other, to hear a guilt which does not give in to shame.

Penelope had issued a sentence of death for herself. She acted according to the neurotic version of death, a deserving death, but one that is never done with. The subject is the agent of death, instead of being subjected to it. We can see a similarity to melancholia (and Penelope was responding to a melancholic mother; she was the shadow of the object over mother's ego). Melancholia is for Freud a sacrifice of the ego in order to keep the loved and hated object, a structure where the subject is placed in the place of an already dead object and where s/he is impotent in front of this *fait accompli*, apart from when s/he breaks into the state of mania. We could say that the melancholic is the sad master of his/her own death. Sadness is for Lacan the effect of a moral cowardice (*lâcheté morale*), a being alive by refusing to become human, by refusing the shame of living humanly. The obsessional instead wishes s/he were the master or mistress of his/her death in order not to face life as shameful. Like Hamlet, the neurotic is guilty to be alive, doubtful whether to be or not to be. His/her crime and shame are his/her life, but like Hamlet and Penelope, s/he lingers on and on before paying for his/her crime; existing. It is this relation of shame to death that gives psychoanalysis its particular ethics of life. This analysis had to wait for the emergence of a structural shame without forcing it, and by revealing the emptiness of her own place, the analyst, like a naive child, points at an obscene nakedness which allows the most solitary feeling of shame.

Time to Conclude

> The man and the woman were both naked, but they did not feel shame . . . God said 'You may eat the fruit of any tree in the garden, except the tree that gives knowledge of what is good and what is bad. You must not eat the fruit of that tree. If you do, you will die the same day.'

This 'dying of shame', then, seems to have a clear biblical reference. And as soon as Adam ate the forbidden fruit which Eve had taken from the tree of knowledge,

> they realized that they were naked; so they sewed fig leaves together and covered themselves . . . The Lord God called out to the man, 'Where are you?'. He answered, 'I heard you in the garden; I was afraid and hid from you, because I was naked'. And God asked 'Who told you that you were naked?'

So, according to the Bible, this primary knowledge entails not only the first loss of innocence but an immediate loss of life. Eating from the tree of life ends the eternal state where there was neither good nor bad, the perfect homeostasis of Nirvana, *the perfect indifference*. The dimension of death was introduced thus in Eden. But what about Adam's and Eve's paradisiac state of ignorance?[1] Is it knowledge that provokes shame at one's own naked ignorance? But Adam and Eve were not supposed to know. *The Other knew for them.* And maybe the snake's fault was not that of lying, but of telling them the truth withheld from them by God, that eating from knowledge makes you wiser, but at the cost of losing your innocence, which is your dependence on the knowledge of the other.

Unlike Lucifer, once the favourite angel of God who sinned for too much knowledge which blinded him by way of arrogance, Eve and Adam, God's favourite creatures, sinned because of ignorance instead. But this ignorance had been dictated by God himself via a threat of death. The biblical paradox is that these primary humans could not sin because they did not know good from bad; they were not supposed to have moral knowledge. Like Oedipus, who did not know that it was his mother he laid, they only knew afterwards that they had done wrong, in the *après coup*. Is there sin where there is no intentionality in sinning? It was only once Adam and Eve ate the fruit that they suddenly knew evil from the good. Only after the introduction of knowledge of moral law did their previously innocent act become a sinful one, the original sin. 'He must not be allowed to eat fruit from the tree of life, and live for ever.' We have a slight change of God's mind at this point from his original threat of immediate death. They will carry on living, but not for ever; the body will die but only until the resurrection of the flesh will give us back our immortal bodies. Man and woman will be saved by God in the end. So to what kind of death is God referring at this point? Not to the death of the body, but to that of the soul. Death is Hell, Lucifer's eternal damnation without appeal, whereas the human damnation is a partial one; we could say a sin 'on probation', as one says of young offenders. In fact, like young offenders, Eve and Adam were still under God's parental responsibility.

Biblically, human life seems to be the result of an attempt to know one's own difference from the Other, to become wiser, as the snake said. One will know by paying in the first person the ransom one needs to pursue one's own desire to know the truth. The payment for breaking the law, whether knowingly or not, is an objective separation from God, and not God's behaviour therapy of punishments and rewards, nor God's revengeful passion. In religious terms it is the 'dogma' which only God knows. In pagan religiosity it was the mystery revealed through a particular experience, that which puts us closer to the unknown. The stress here is on reunion rather than the original, ignorant union with Him. The human, for the Bible, is born of this very fall or separation from the Other. Life, after the expulsion from paradise, will be this probation, this attempt to find the Other again, not as a punishing judge but as a saviour. This is the quintessential Christian optimism. But the Bible is implicitly a dualistic doctrine. There is God, with his omnipotence, but the evil is right there in the middle of God's 'green paradise', ready to swallow up his creatures. This evil splits God himself, gives a limit to his omnipotence.[2] The Christian solution is that the potence of God is made operative only by way of love. God loves his imperfect creatures, and only their love for him will save them. It is this reciprocal love which is achieved in the mystical encounter, and the effect of this achieved reunion is religious initiation.

Initiation into any religion is an attempt to recuperate a friendship with God. The ancient religious sacrifice has always been the way humans pay the gods for the protection effected by their love. In the mysteric rite too it is a demon which comes to hurt you as soon as the 'golden calf', the phallus, the earthly power, is being revealed to you, as soon as you think that knowledge is now in your possession. So the initiation is not the revelation in itself but its effects: the separating whip, the expulsion from the divine union, and the re-rising of the flesh in the dancing Bacchant, the culmination of the initiatory effect. Initiation does not involve just the revelation of a reunion with God but also the revelation of a traumatic separation from him. A sacrifice is always entailed in our relation to the Other.

This whipping, this painful expulsion, this loss is part of the analytical progression too. Freud picked out the phantasy of 'A child is being beaten'. Of all phantasies of his patients, this was the one he wrote a paper about (1919). Lacan read this phantasy as a 'fundamental phantasy' which becomes crucial in determining the end of analysis. It is the crossing of a fixed point of horror and humiliation, which are clothed in a variety of unconscious phantasies. The phantasy is the point of absolute resistance to knowledge (*savoir*). It is the resistance of the 'real' to the symbolic. Not-all speaks, but 'some' enjoys, even at the cost of a good beating. If the signifier, as we have seen it operating in the clinical cases, is the means of the subject's mobility, thanks to which s/he can become in space and in time, the phantasy comes back to the same place timelessly; it is the reservoir of forbidden enjoyment which analysis will have crossed in the end.

The dancing Bacchant and the eyes of the bride at the mirror (plates 7 and 8) are not ecstatic images such as the union of the divine couple, but they express earthly pleasure, the recuperation of one's own flesh separated from the Other's. The little Eroses, a desire for love, are what the initiate is left with. For the Pompeian brides this was their initiation into their wifely love. The Bacchanalia were probably an initiation into love for earthly people.

In his last, unpublished seminar, 'La topologie et le temps', Lacan makes his last rite of veiling-unveiling. He confesses something he had meant not to confess, that all his mathematical unveiling was only imaginary, and therefore 'does not go very far'.

> There is a *'forcage'* [forcing] which is called initiation. Psychoanalysis is an anti-initiation.[3] The initiation is that by which one can elevate oneself, if I can say so, to the Phallus. It is not easy to know what is initiation and what is not. But in the end the general orientation is that the Phallus has to be integrated. It is necessary that in the absence of initiation one is either man or woman . . . as a third sex cannot subsist in the presence of the other two.

These last words come to confirm his early ones in 'The mirror stage', that 'it is not in our power as practitioners to bring him to that point where the real journey [initiation] begins' (1977d, p. 7). But he seems also to reveal a certain disappointment at this confirmation, as if somewhere else he would have liked the phallus revealed at last, as if he believed in an elevation to it through psychoanalysis, somehow, in the end.

But what he found himself unveiling in his work was not the phallic idol, but the nothing of the feminine encounter with God, there where there would be sexual rapport, but only beyond the phallic distinction of the sexes. It is this nothing which Lacan unveiled, and which makes one almost die of shame; it is what really initiates one into the human quest. And this is not the quest of the few; like the Dionysiac rites, the analytical unveiling initiates the many, those who want to carry on living to make sense of death which life entails. The mysteric revelation was exactly this experience of elevation and dejection, which aims at 'integrating' this phallus. There is no elevation to the phallus, which is only the emblem of human power and human fall. Psychoanalysis aims at this integration of the human, a necessary step for any possible elevation. This is the Dionysiac and the psychoanalytical initiation. But, as for a mystical elevation to the Other's potence, as for having it revealed at last, yes, that is beyond psychoanalysis.

Notes

Preface

1 Interesting work has been done by an anthropologist and a psychoanalyst together in a New Guineas' tribe on eroticism and its rites of passage (Herdt and Stoller, 1990).

A note on the ancient mysteries

1 After the last earthquake in Naples in 1980 the earth kept quaking lightly for years, in conjunction with bradyseisms (progressive lowerings of the earth), in the nearby village of Pozzuoli, which was evacuated and held the attention of seismologists worldwide.

2 It is important here to point out at least two of Dionysus' possible origins. First, the god is seen as the child of Samele, the daughter of the king of Thebes, and Zeus. Or secondly, the identification of Dionysus with the Cretan god Zagreus sees the god as originating from Orphic mysteries. Dionysus/Zagreus was, in fact, the son of Zeus and either Demeter or Kore/Persephone, her daughter, goddess of the earth and of the Eleusinian mysteries from which derive the Dionysiac ones.

3 In contrast with Apollo, the conservative god who moved in the higher circles of the establishment, the Dionysiac approach is a subversive one. Dionysiac culture is the one enhanced either by the many (the mass madness of Bacchanalia or Maenadism) or the very few (the mysteries' esotericism). A comparison could be made with Marxism or the drug culture at their origins, and their development into mass phenomena under certain circumstances. There are times, as in a revolution, when the subversive aspects of an elite become social subversion. The safe eccentricity of the few spreads to the powerful majority.

4 This feminine character was certainly the model for the ideal of another Diotima, the Domina of the 'Collateral Campaign' (congress of

great ideas) in Robert Musil's *The Man Without Qualities* (1954). The Austrian Diotima failed because she did not dominate herself; she fell in love with her initiate Arnheim like a patient in transference, a long way away from the end of an initiation! In its encounter with the West, the East too is producing women gurus. A good account of a contemporary initiation by the light of the seventeen-year-old Mother Meera has been written by A. Harvey (1991).

5   The idea that this is a mother–son relationship does not contradict the more widely accepted interpretation of a pre-nuptial initiation for the brides-to-be. In fact the Eleusinian mysteries were celebrated in honour of Demeter, who was also goddess of marriage. Something similar to this transmission of knowledge from mother to son is encountered in George Bataille's novel *Ma Mère*, where the mother initiates her grown-up young son into her ministry of Eros (Bataille, 1988).

6   In more Freudian terms, panic comes from the lost paradise of childhood's polymorphous sexuality. (We shall come back to the Lacanian cause as the object which *causes* desire rather than being the *object of* desire.)

7   For Mudie-Cook (1913), it is the scene of 'lekanomanzia', divination by means of a cup full of water, or, as for Macchioro (1920), 'catoptromanzia', divination by means of vases and deforming mirrors.

8   Maiuri describes the couple in terms of the god and his wife Ariadne in the celebration of their marriage. The fact that the woman's face is lost keeps the enigma of her identity intact.

9   One cannot help being struck by the similarity of the posture with that of the holy couple so much represented in Catholic art: the Pietà, Christ's body in the arms of his mother Mary. Maybe it is only as a dead body that Christ can enjoy his mother, who could not initiate him into life, since his life was possessed by the initiation at the hands of the Father.

10 Dionysus is the god on earth and of joy today, somewhat like that which Julian Beck, Dionysiac apologist in the sixties, expressed in his theatrical happening *Paradise Now*. Dionysus has learned godly love from his mother. He is the god who enjoys like a woman, and the god of women, and their divine lover. He initiates women into their own enjoyment, and only women can initiate men into the Dionysiac 'feminine' enjoyment.

11 Rizzo (1914) translates Aidos as Modesty. But here there is more than a young bride's simple modesty. A flagellator is barring the sight of the Phallus as if even a fleeting glimpse of it seems to deserve shame.

12 We shall see later how this ritual of pain and purification in the phallic rites of the Greek Dionysiac cult resembles the Freudian phantasy 'A child is being beaten' (Freud, 1919) and what will become, for Lacan,

the regularity of the sadomasochist fundamental phantasy. It is by going through this phallic whipping that maternity as symbolic fecundity is given to the bride-to-be. Leader (1992) has pointed out Lehmann's (1962) interpretation of the demon as Αγνοια, Ignorance, which is a very suggestive idea. Ignorance is, after all, together with love and hate, a passion, the passion of not wanting to know which underlies the resistance to analysis.

13 The Dionysiac approach to the divinity is a mass event fuelled by its sacred elements of wine and dance. In Dodds's theory (1951) the phenomenon of Maenadism entails a collective possession, a ritual outlet of irrational impulses in the Archaic age of a shame culture rather than a later guilt culture. The Bacchanalia would not have been very dissimilar to the cathartic function of ritual madness in the current secret 'Ecstasy parties', where young people rave and dance exactly in the Maenad fashion. In fact, far from being a matter for the few, the Dionysiac rituals were a mass event and were pursued for their own sake as mental and spiritual healing. Deleuze (1965) has pointed out how the Dionysiac and Apolline, in spite of the Nietzschian distinction, are the two indissoluble aspects of the Greek search for religious knowledge. The Apolline aims at knowledge via divination whereas the Dionysiac rituals aimed at knowledge of and as ecstasy. In contrast to Dionysiac popularity, in spite of the secret mysteries, Apollo moved in higher societies in search of ethical sobriety (Greek rationalism), and the gift of initiation was for the few, the exceptional individuals. But this does not prevent, as Deleuze points out, Apolline priestesses such as Cassandra and the Sybil from having ecstatic encounters with the god, who would possess their bodies.

14 Are not Catholic churches an exhibition of the torments of the flesh of Christ and his martyrs, whose sacred 'enjoyment' the Christian eye secretly enjoys?

Chapter 1   A discourse on love

1 The difference in French between *savoir* and *connaissance*, which does not exist in English, is crucial in understanding the difference between a knowledge of things which are definable within language (*connaissance*) and a knowledge which is banned from definitions (*savoir*). The latter can enter our discourse only in code, as in dreams, or by interference, as in slips of the tongue, etc. *Savoir* is, in a broad sense, unconscious knowledge.

2 When I went recently to a family planning clinic for a routine cervical smear I was also handed a pile of condoms and instructed minutely on how to use them. 'You do not leave it to men, women must make sure

it is done properly', the safe sex expert was telling me, while handling skilfully with her aseptic hand a sizeable plastic penis. 'Sorry for the straightforwardness', the salvation sex lady went on, while slipping a pamphlet into my hands. It was only once I was out in the street and threw a glance at the pamphlet that I felt embarrassed. The pamphlet contained a series of pictures illustrating how you get a perfectly erect penis condomed. My embarrassment alerted me to the fact that what I had read a minute earlier as hygienic instructions had now become, in a different context, pure pornography. So many ways to read a hard prick.

3   The reader will find the whole commentary on this case in chapter 7.

4   The reader will find a detailed commentary on Dora's case in part II of this book.

5   I have used the English word 'enjoyment' in most of the book as a coarse translation of the French word '*jouissance*', which Lacan has introduced into the French psychoanalytical vocabulary, and which has been adopted by other languages as well. The problem that this translation poses is the everyday use of this term in English. 'Sexual enjoyment', which I have used several times in the text when appropriate, restricts the meaning of the French word, which, even though it includes sexuality, is an enjoyment which goes beyond it. The enjoyment involved in *jouissance* goes beyond pleasure as well. This is the reason why I use the French term *jouissance* from time to time; it is a way to remind the reader of the very specific meaning of the *Lacanian enjoyment* which perhaps only the French word really conveys. *Jouissance* stands for that specific part of sexual enjoyment which overrides the boundaries of the Pleasure Principle. *Jouissance* is, therefore, painful at the level of the symptom.

6   The word 'instinct' that is used in the English translation of Freud is inadequate for a Lacanian reading, which adopts the word 'drive' (pulsion) to underline the 'wildness' of the Freudian primordial force; that is, without a specific object as its aim. The Freudian '*Trieb*' is not a biological instinct (hunger, sex), whose goal (food) does not coincide with its aim. Survival is not an instinct but quite the contrary, an anti-instinct, the artful erotic binding, a suspension of an unrestrained force (the driving factor).

7   I associate this 'going on living' with the words the Wolf-man's mother addressed to her doctor: 'I can't go on living like this', with which the Wolf-man identified in his symptoms (Freud, 1918).

8   M. Bowe (1987) has commented on Proust's 'impassioned' discourse of love.

9   I refer the reader to the chapter on the Mirror Stage in Benvenuto and Kennedy (1986).

10 The possession of the object, that is, of the piece of the body of the

lover, corresponds to his disappearance and her madness. This particular discourse of love unfolds in the context of a war which is waged in the background; the two lovers try to place themselves outside it, in vain. Their radical love-making is a discourse of war on the reverse side. Whereas they refuse to play the social games of domination and possession of the enemy, they choose a similarly sacrificial game on the erotic, binding side!

11 I have chosen this particular modern English translation where 'Honour thy father and thy mother' is replaced by the more current and meaningful 'Respect'.

12 We will see in chapter 3 how this is the background of passions.

13 The Lacanian term 'real' indicates precisely the dimension of this *jouissance* – what resides beyond the limits of symbolization and representation, the exhaustion of any lack and suspension. And the body is the battlefield of all three orders, like the bodies of the Japanese lovers. As the carrier of the imaginary object, the body seduces us, while it frightens us in the 'real', and binds us together only when it is kept at a respectful distance in the symbolic.

14 I am indebted to Susanne Lilar for her two very beautiful books: *Le couple* (1963), for her commentaries on and quotes from Hadewijch d'Anvers; and *La confession anonyme* (1983). The quotations from Hadewijch are my translation.

15 'It was on a Sunday of the eighth pentecost that our Lord was secretly brought to my bed, because I was feeling in great trouble inside my soul, which I could not have felt outside, among people. And the demand I had within myself was to be one with God and enjoy him' (van Mierlo, 1924: my translation).

16 Socrates was condemned to death because of his subversive mysticism, which even the democratic Athens was not able to integrate. I disagree with Stone (1989), who claims that Socrates was condemned for not being democratic enough, for being a betrayer of democracy. Socrates was laying down the principles of a culture to come.

17 'The Woman does not exist' was one of Lacan's most controversial statements, which has provoked a very fertile debate in the French and worldwide feminist movement. On this argument I refer you to chapters 4 and 5.

Chapter 2   What is the psychoanalyst supposed to know?

1 For a phenomenology of shame see chapter 10.

2 'Forclusion' is how Lacan translated the Freudian '*Verwerfung*'; that is, the radical psychotic rejection of a primordial meaning (or signifier), as

different from repression, which is the typically neurotic condemning and burying of unconscious ideas.

3   This case is published in J. Lacan's first seminar (1954–5), now translated into English (1987).

4   Here meaning translates the more fluid 'sens', and not 'signification' which is a fixed meaning.

5   The word 'formation' in English does not render the same meaning as in French. *Formation* hardly corresponds to the English 'training' which offers official recognition according to fixed rules and criteria. *Formation* indicates a subjective process that stretches well beyond a training.

Chapter 3   The passion of childhood

1   This is the position of the 'beautiful soul', the one who condemns the disorder of the world, a disorder which starts from within him/herself. We will see in part II how the hysteric represents well the Hegelian 'belle âme'.

2   This case was discussed by Lacan (1987).

3   For Françoise Dolto also the image of the mother's body plays an important role in the child's psyche's set-up, but with very different clinical consequences (Dolto, 1984; Dolto and Nasio, 1992).

4   The logical time includes three moments: (1) the moment to look; (2) the moment to understand; (3) the moment to conclude. Analytical time is not chronological (the unconscious is timeless) but a series of scansions in the process of acknowledgement.

5   This is a different way to conceive counter-transference. Transference in analysis involves both analyst and analysand, and what takes place between them is 'transferential interaction'.

6   This is our *jouissance*, our death drive. This is passion in its clinical phenomenology. I will not investigate here the relationship of passion with death drive, of passion as a coercion to repeat a primary *jouissance*.

7   As for a specific prematurity of birth in humans, see Lacan (1977d, p. 4) and B. Benvenuto (1989, pp. 414–15).

8   He commented on such an encounter magnificently in the terms of the tragedy of Antigone, in his seminar on the ethics of psychoanalysis (1986).

Interlude

1 The Lacanian subject is in French *'parl-être'* which, in English, corresponds to something like 'speaking being'.
2 The dialogues between these texts are excerpts from an unpublished paper co-written with Sergio Benvenuto.
3 $$\frac{\text{knowledge}}{\text{senses}} = \frac{\text{symbolic}}{\text{feelings}}$$

Chapter 4 Hysteria: Comedy . . . *dell'Arte*

1 A Lacanian overview on feminine sexuality has been given in Benvenuto and Kennedy (1986), chapter 10.
2 *Lazzi*, a Lombardian expression for 'knots', were the jests and tricks of the Italian improvisers of the *commedia dell'arte*. They were used widely in European comedy, from Molière to Shakespeare. See Duchartre (1966).

Chapter 5 Compliance and disagreement

An original version of this text was presented at the conference 'Sexual difference', Southampton, 1986.
1 We shall discuss Freud's comments on Anderson's tale 'The emperor's new clothes' in chapter 10.
2 When this text was written Aids had not appeared yet and therefore its mark and its significance in the development of sexual devices are not commented on here. But this analysis can still hold as background to the Aids phenomenon.
3 Lévy's opinion, in his *Le testament de Dieu* (1979), is that only the monotheist god is the guarantor of the law, whereas the pagan gods are gods of havoc and disorder. Lévy sees God also as split and lacking (the Lacanian axiom $\cancel{A}$ also assumes a lack in the Other, who is, therefore, not absolute). In defence of this 'different' god, he regards paganism as an inferior form of both religiosity and law: arbitrary and tyrannical. It is in this respect that Lacan too corrects Freud in his flight into paganism. Lacan reintroduces (unveils?) Freud's monotheistic unconscious (but in its Catholic form) into psychoanalysis's pagan mythology. The phallus and the Name of the Father coexist in Lacan in the same way as Domina and the phallus coexist but are not the same. Lévy, on the other hand, preaches about the split in monotheism, but cannot see the pagan aspect of it.

4   For the discussion of the two great debates on femininity see Teresa Brennan (1992).
5   More detailed comments on Dora's case are in chapter 6.

Chapter 6   The paradoxes of the earthly woman

1   I use here the word 'transference' in the wide sense of 'love for the one who is supposed to know', which is applicable, before the analyst, to the relation to any authority, which is by definition supposed to know the law. It applies mainly to the doctor (Latin *'doctum'* means learned, knowledgeable, one who has this hypnotic quality).
2   The scene on the lake is now famous because of Lacan's (1966d) translation of Mr K.'s words, 'I get nothing out of my wife' in the English translation (Freud, 1905a, p. 106), into 'My wife is nothing for me.' In both cases the 'nothing' is the 'thing' which either a woman is or one gets out of her.
3   We will see in chapter 8, in Winnicott's case, how the little Piggle stages her own birth from her father's head. As I mention there, Eric Laurent (1981) calls it the myth of Athena, who was born from the darkness of her father's head.
4   A pun on *objet petit* (a) and 'no-thing'.
5   Hence the formula 'The Woman (what of a woman accedes to the 'real') does not exist.' She is not-all in the 'real' (she is not all-Woman, she is not all-inexistent) but she is not-all in the symbolic either (she is not all-Man).

Chapter 8   Winnicott's 'Piggle'

1   In perversion, too, there is an object at stake, but this is the imaginary phallus of the mother. The perverse preserves this lacking object as a fetish by identifying with it. The perverse is in the position of the maternal object, of her phallus. But this primary maternal omnipotence which the infant shared and lost was not the phallus, which is only a simulacrum of what is not there, namely, the object *a*.
2   This is 'enjoyment' in the English sense of participation. It is nothing like *jouissance* that he is intentionally talking about here, even though it is clear throughout the case that Winnicott is very sensitive to things like 'a generalized orgasm'.

Chapter 10   To die of shame

1   As J. Hyppolite (1966) has pointed out in his commentary on Freud's *Verneinung* in Lacan's *Ecrits, Aufhebung* is the Hegelian dialectical word, whose fundamental meaning is 'lifting', but at one and the same time it means 'denying', 'suppressing' and 'preserving'. For Freud, negation is this lifting of the repressed through a suppression and a preservation of it. To deny is a form of negative judgement of something which nevertheless has been accepted as existing. A victory of the life desire!

2   'The phallus is the signifier of this *Aufhebung* itself, which it inaugurates (initiates) by its disappearance. That is why the demon of Αἰδώς (*Scham* shame) arises at the very moment when, in the ancient mysteries, the phallus is unveiled. It then becomes the bar which, at the hands of this demon, strikes the signified, marking it as the bastard offspring of this signifying concatenation' (Lacan, 1977e, p. 288).

3   I translated these excerpts from an original transcription of *L'envers de la psychanalyse* (Lacan, 1991b) before its recent publication.

4   'The original manner of eliding a signifier, which we are trying to conceive here as the matrix of 'Verneinung', affirms the subject in a negative manner, while managing the emptiness in which it finds its place' (Lacan, 1966b, pp. 665–6: trans. CFAR).

5   'This absence of the subject, which is produced somewhere in the unorganised Id, is the defence one could call natural, however tainted by artifice the circle, burnt in the veld of the drives in order to offer the other agencies a place to camp and organise theirs' (Lacan, 1966b, p. 666).

Time to conclude

1   We can see here how Lehmann's (1962) Daemon of Ignorance links to shame.

2   The Other is always a barred Other. Even in God there is a lack, a point of difference from himself.

3   I am not sure if Lacan's term 'anti-initiation', as it was transcribed from his last, unpublished seminar, could be heard as 'ante-initiation', as a preceding state, as what has to have happened before any possible initiation.

Bibliography

Aries, P. (1979) *Centuries of Childhood*. Harmondsworth: Penguin.

Barnes, M. and Berke, J. (1971) *Mary Barnes: two accounts of a journey through madness*. London: MacGibbon & Kee.

Barthes, R. (1978) *A Lover's Discourse*. New York: Hill & Wang.

Bataille, G. (1988) *My Mother, Madame Edwarda, the Dead Man*. London: Manon Boyars.

de Beauvoir, S. (1972) *The Second Sex*. Harmondsworth: Penguin. First published 1949.

Benvenuto, B. (1986) Compliance and disagreement. *Oxford Literary Review*, 8. 'Sexual Difference', 28–34.

Benvenuto, B. (1989) Once upon a time: the infant in the Lacanian theory. *British Journal of Psychotherapy*, 5, 3, 409–22.

Benvenuto, B. and Kennedy, R. (1986) *The Works of Jacques Lacan: an introduction*. London: Free Association Books.

Benvenuto, S. (1991) Psychoanalysis and hermeneutics. *Differentia: Review of Italian Thought*, V, 79–90.

Bernheimer, C. and Kahane, C., eds (1985) *In Dora's Case: Freud, hysteria and feminism*. New York: Columbia University Press.

Bion, W. (1970) *Attention and Interpretation*. London: Tavistock Press.

Bion, W. (1980) *Bion in New York and Sao Paulo*. Perthshire: Clunie Press.

Bowe, M. (1987) *Freud, Proust and Lacan: theory as fiction*. Cambridge: Cambridge University Press.

Brennan, T. (1992) *The Interpretation of the Flesh*. London: Routledge.

Breuer, J. and Freud, S. (1893) Studies on hysteria. In Standard Edition, vol. II, London: Hogarth Press.

Burkert, W. (1987) *Ancient Mystery Cults*. Cambridge, MA: Harvard University Press.

Carter, A. (1979) *The Sadeian Woman: an exercise in cultural history*. London: Virago.

Deleuze, G. (1965) *Nietzsche*. Paris: Presses Universitaires de France.

Derrida, J. (1976) *Grammatology*. Trans. S.C. Spivak. Baltimore: Johns Hopkins.

Derrida, J. (1987) *The Postcard: from Socrates to Freud and beyond*. Trans. A. Bass, Chicago: University of Chicago Press.

Derrida, J. (1990) Cogito and history of madness. In *Writing and Difference*, trans. A. Bass, Routledge.

Derrida, J. (1991) Pour l'amour de Lacan. In *Lacan avec les philosophes*, Paris: Albin Michel.

Descartes, R. (1984) Meditations on first philosophy. In *The Philosophical Writings of Descartes*, vol. 2, Cambridge: Cambridge University Press.

Didi-Huberman, G. (1982) *L'Invention de l'Hysterie: Charcot et l'iconographie de la Selpetrière*. Paris: Macula.

Dodds, E.R. (1951) *The Greeks and the Irrational*. London: University of California Press.

Dolto, F. (1984) *L'image inconsciente du corps*. Paris: Seuil.

Dolto, F. and Nasio, J.D. (1992) *L'enfants du miroir*. Paris: Payot.

Duchartre, P.L. (1966) *The Italian Comedy*. New York: Dover.

Dunand, A. (1988) Commentaire de Hadewijch. *Ornicar? (Review du Champ freudien)*, 47, 21–33.

Fairbairn, W.R.D. (1952) *Psychoanalytic Studies of the Personality*. London: Tavistock Press.

Foucault, M. (1971) *Madness and Civilisation: a history of insanity in the Age of Reason*.

Foucault, M. (1976–84) *Histoire de la sexualité. Vol. I: La volonté de savoir. Vol. II: L'usage des plaisirs. Vol. III: Le souci de soi*. Paris: Gallimard.

Freud, S. (1900) The interpretation of dreams. In Standard Edition, vol. 4, London: Hogarth Press.

Freud, S. (1905a) Fragment of an analysis of a case of hysteria. In Standard Edition, vol. 7, London: Hogarth Press.

Freud, S. (1905b) Three essays on the Theory of Sexuality. In Standard Edition, vol. 7, London: Hogarth Press.

Freud, S. (1905c) Jokes and their relation to the unconscious. In Standard Edition, vol. 8, London: Hogarth Press.

Freud, S. (1909) Analysis of a phobia in a five-year-old boy. In Standard Edition, vol. 10, London: Hogarth Press.

Freud, S. (1911a) Formulations on the two principles of mental functioning. In Standard Edition, vol. 12, London: Hogarth Press.

Freud, S. (1911b) Psychoanalytical notes on an autobiographical account of a case of paranoia (*Dementia Paranoides*). In Standard Edition, vol. 12, London: Hogarth Press.

Freud, S. (1913) Totem and taboo. In Standard Edition, vol. 13, London: Hogarth Press.

Freud, S. (1914) On narcissism: an introduction. In Standard Edition, vol. 14, London: Hogarth Press.

Freud, S. (1918) From the history of an infantile neurosis. In Standard Edition, vol. 17, London: Hogarth Press.

Freud, S. (1919) A child is being beaten: a contribution to the study of the origin of sexual perversion. In Standard Edition, vol. 17, London: Hogarth Press.

Freud, S. (1920a) Beyond the pleasure principle. In Standard Edition, vol. 18, London: Hogarth Press.

Freud, S. (1920b) The psychogenesis of a case of homosexuality in a woman. In Standard Edition, vol. 18, London: Hogarth Press.

Freud, S. (1923) The ego and the id. In Standard Edition, vol. 19, London: Hogarth Press.

Freud, S. (1926) Inhibitions, symptoms and anxiety. In Standard Edition, vol. 20, London: Hogarth Press.

Freud, S. (1930) Civilization and its discontents. In Standard Edition, vol. 21, London: Hogarth Press.

Hadewijch d'Anvers (1985) *Ecrits mystiques des Béguines*. Trans. J.-B.P. Paris: Seuil.

Harvey, A. (1991) *Hidden Journey*. London: Bloomsbury.

Hegel, G.W.F. (1967) *The Phenomenology of Mind*. New York: Harper.

Heidegger, M. (1954) *What is Called Thinking?* New York: Harper and Row.

Herdt, G. and Stoller, R.J. (1990) *Intimate Communications: erotics and the study of culture*. New York: Columbia University Press.

Hyppolite, J. (1966) Commentaire parlé sur la 'Verneinung' de Freud. In J. Lacan, *Ecrits*, Paris: Seuil.

Jong, E. (1974) *Fear of Flying*. London: Secker & Warburg.

Jong, E. (1977) *How to Save Your Own Life*. London: Secker & Warburg.

Klein, M. (1932) On symbol formation. In *The Psychoanalysis of Children*, London: Hogarth Press.

Klein, M. (1961) *The Narrative of a Child Analysis*. London: Hogarth Press.

Klein, M. (1975) *Envy and Gratitude and Other Works, 1946/63*. London: Hogarth Press and the Institute of Psychoanalysis.

Lacan, J. (1956–7) La relation d'objet et les structures freudiennes. Summaries of Lacan's Seminar 1956–7. *Bulletin de Psychologie*, 7t. x, 426–30; 10, 602–5; 12, 742–3; 14, 851–4.

Lacan, J. (1966a) *Au-delà du principe de réalité*. Paris: Seuil. First published 1936.

Lacan, J. (1966b) Remarque sur le rapport de Daniel Lagache: 'Psycho-analyse et la structure de la personalité'. In *Ecrits*, Paris: Seuil. First published 1961.

Lacan, J. (1966c) Le temps logique et l'assertion de certitude anticipée. In *Ecrits*, Paris: Seuil. First published 1944.

Lacan, J. (1966d) Intervention sur le transfert. In *Ecrits*, Paris: Seuil. First published 1952.

Lacan, J. (1975) *Le Seminaire 20: encore* (1972–3). Paris: Seuil.

Lacan, J. (1977a) The agency of the letter in the unconscious, or reason since Freud. In *Ecrits: a Selection*, London: Tavistock Press.

Lacan, J. (1977b) Aggressivity in psychoanalysis. In *Ecrits: a Selection*, London: Tavistock Press. First published 1948.

Lacan, J. (1977c) *The Four Fundamental Concepts of Psychoanalysis*. London: Hogarth Press.

Lacan, J. (1977d) The mirror stage as formative of the function of the I as revealed in psychoanalytical experience. In *Ecrits: a Selection*, London: Tavistock Press. First published 1949.

Lacan, J. (1977e) The signification of the Phallus. In *Ecrits: a Selection*, London: Tavistock Press. First published 1958.

Lacan, J. (1986) *Le Seminaire 7: l'ethique de la psychanalyse* (1959–60). Paris: Seuil.

Lacan, J. (1987) *The Seminar of Jacques Lacan. Book 1: Freud's Papers on Technique 1953–1954*. Cambridge: Cambridge University Press.

Lacan, J. (1991a) *Le Seminaire 8: le transfert* (1960–1). Paris: Seuil. First published 1960.

Lacan, J. (1991b) *Le Seminaire 17: l'envers de la psychanalyse* (1969–70). Paris: Seuil.

Laurent, E. (1981) *Lire Gabrielle et Richard a partir du Petit Hans*. Brussels: Quarto.

Leader, D. (1992) *Etudes lacaniennes autour de la Comedie*. Paris: Université de Paris VIII.

Lefort, R. and Lefort, R. (1980) *Naissance de l'autre*. Paris: Seuil.

Lefort, R. and Lefort, R. (1988) *Les Structures de la Psychose*. Paris: Seuil. E.d.S.

Lehmann, K. (1962) Ignorance and search in the Villa of the Mysteries. *Journal of Roman Studies*, vol. 52, pp. 62–8.

Lemoine-Luccioni, E. (1976) *The Dividing of Women, or Woman's Lot*. London: Free Association Books.

Lemoine-Luccioni, E. (1987) *Psychoanalyse pour la vie quotidienne*. Paris: Navarin.

Lévy, B.H. (1979) *Le testament de Dieu*. Paris: Grasset & Fasquelle.

Lilar, S. (1963) *Le couple*. Paris: Bernard Grasset.

Lilar, S. (1983) *La confession anonyme*. Paris: Gallimard.

Macchioro, V. (1920) *Zagreus: Studi sull'Orfismo*. Turin: Atti Accademia.

Maiuri, A. (1931) *La Villa dei Misteri*. Rome: La Libreria dello Stato.

McDougall, J. (1986) *Theatres of the Mind: illusion and truth on the psychoanalytic stage*. London: Free Association Books.

Meltzer, D. (1978) *The Kleinian Development, Part 2*. Perthshire: Clunie Press.

Meltzer, D. (1984) *Dream-life: a re-examination of the psycho-analytical theory and technique*. Perthshire: Clunie Press.

van Mierlo, S.J. (1924) *Visioenen*. Lavanio.

Millot, C. (1988) *Nobodaddy: l'hysterie dans le siècle*. Paris; Point Hors Ligne.

Mitchell, J. (1975) *Psychoanalysis and Feminism.* Harmondsworth: Pelican.

Mitchell, J. and Rose, J. (1982) *Feminine Sexuality: Jacques Lacan and the 'Ecole Freudienne'.* London: Macmillan.

Mudie-Cook, P.B. (1913) The paintings of the Villa Item at Pompeii. *Journal of Roman Studies,* 3, 157–74.

Musil, R. (1954) *The Man Without Qualities.* London: Picador.

Nillson, M.P. (1957) *The Dionysiac Mysteries of the Hellenistic and Roman Age.* Lund: Acta Instituti Atheniensis Regni Sueciae.

Ogden, C.K. and Richards, I.A. (1985) *Meaning of Meaning: study of the influence of language upon thought and on the science of symbolism.* London: Arc.

Plato (1951) *The Symposium.* Harmondsworth: Penguin.

Reich, W. (1973) *The Function of the Orgasm: sex-economic problems of biological energy.* New York: Farrar, Straus and Giroux.

Rizzo, G.G. (1914) *Dionysos Mystes, contributi esegetici alle rappresentazioni di misteri orfici.* Naples: Memorie della Reale Accademia di Archeologia.

Rumi, J. (1979) *The Masnavi: teachings of Rumi.* London: Sufi Trust.

Rushdie, S. (1982) *Midnight's Children.* London: Picador.

Safouan, M. (1976) *La sexualité féminine.* Paris: Seuil.

Safouan, M. (1983) *Jacques Lacan et la question de la formation des analystes.* Paris: Seuil.

Segal, H. (1986) *A Kleinian Approach to Clinical Practice: delusion and artistic creativity and other psychoanalytic essays.* London: Free Association Books.

Stone, I.F. (1989) *The Trial of Socrates.* London: Picador.

Toynbee, J. (1929) The Villa Item and a bride's ordeal. *Journal of Roman Studies,* 19, 67–87.

Winnicott, D.W. (1971) Mirror-role of mother and family in child development. In *Playing and Reality,* London: Tavistock Press.

Winnicott, D.W. (1989) *The Piggle.* London: Pelican. First published 1977.

Wittgenstein, L. (1953) *Philosophical Investigations.* Oxford: Blackwell & Mott.

Index

imaginary: in Klein and Lacan,
34–7
infants *see* child analysis; children
initiation, 149–50
injection of the symbolic, 117
invention, 27

jokes, 69–70, 130
Jong, Erica
Fear of Flying, 15
How to Save Your Own Life, 15
jouissance see enjoyment, sexual

Klein, Madeleine, 31
father, 98
infantile development, 34–7,
42–3, 45, 110, 137
Little Dick, 35
Richard, 116–26
knowledge
and psychoanalysis, 23–30,
32–4, 80
and sexuality, 84
and shame, 147–8
and truth, 139

Lacan, J., 31, 49–50, 53, 56, 141
absence, 133
being, 55
infantile development, 34–7,
42–5, 124
Little Hans, 104
love, 11, 12, 15–16
Mirror Stage, 44, 82–3
nature of femininity, 62, 63
parents, 98, 109
phallus, 101, 135
psychoanalysis, xvii, 6, 66, 139,
149
sadness, 146
sexuality, 19, 22, 79
split subject, 24, 134
symbolic castration, 99
unconscious, 33–4

unveiling, 150
language
and existence, 63
and hysteria, 66
and identity, 88–9
and love, 10, 18–19
and sexuality, 72–3
slips of the tongue, 130
of the unconscious, 24–6, 117
Laurent, Eric, 113
law of the father, 27–8, 43, 45
Lefort, R.: wolf-child case, 25–6
libido, 61, 68, 79
life drive: and love, 6, 7–10
literature: love in, 14–15, 16
love, x
and desire, 89–90
discourse on, 3–22
mystic, 15–20, 21, 147–50
and passion, 46–7
platonic, 12–14, 81–2

Macchiorro, V., xiv
McDougall, J., 40
madness, 49–56
Mary Barnes case, 66–8
Maiuri, A., xiv, xv–xvi
Marx, Karl, 56
masochism, 137
master-slave couple, 28, 104
mastery: and knowledge, 139–40
melancholia, 146
Meltzer, D., 45, 123–4
men: sexuality, 19–20
mirror images, 87
Mirror Stage, 44, 82–3
Mitchell, Juliet, 73
morality, 129
mothers and mothering, xvi
Dora, 83–4, 96
Little Hans, 99–101
Penelope, 141–6
Piggle, 109–11, 112, 113–14
pre-Oedipal, 97–8